HOT TOPICS

W9-AUE-305

HEALTH CARE
LIMITS, LAWS, AND LIVES AT STAKE

By Tyler Stevenson

Portions of this book originally appeared in *Health Care* by Debra A. Miller.

LUCENT
P R E S S

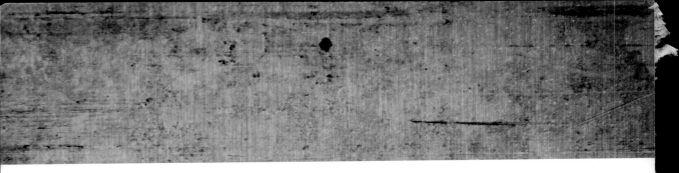

Published in 2019 by
Lucent Press, an Imprint of Greenhaven Publishing, LLC
353 3rd Avenue
Suite 255
New York, NY 10010

Designer: Andrea Davison-Bartolotta and Deanna Paternostro
Editor: Jennifer Lombardo

Library of Congress Cataloging-in-Publication Data

Names: Stevenson, Tyler (Tyler Dennis), 1988- author.
Title: Health care : limits, laws, and lives at stake / Tyler Stevenson.
Description: New York : Lucent Press, 2019. | Series: Hot topics | Includes
  bibliographical references and index.
Identifiers: LCCN 2018004325 (print) | LCCN 2018002142 (ebook) | ISBN
  9781534563483 (eBook) | ISBN 9781534563476 (library bound book) | ISBN
  9781534563490 (pbk. book)
Subjects: LCSH: Health care reform–United States. | Medical policy–United
  States. | Health insurance–Law and legislation–United States.
Classification: LCC RA395.A3 (print) | LCC RA395.A3 S818 2019 (ebook) | DDC
  362.1/0425–dc23
LC record available at https://lccn.loc.gov/2018004325

Printed in the United States of America

CPSIA compliance information: Batch #BS18KL: For further information contact Greenhaven Publishing LLC, New York, New
York at 1-844-317-7404.

Please visit our website, www.greenhavenpublishing.com. For a free color catalog of all our
high-quality books, call toll free 1-844-317-7404 or fax 1-844-317-7405.

CONTENTS

Adolescence is a time when many people begin to take notice of the world around them. News channels, blogs, and talk radio shows are constantly promoting one view or another; very few are unbiased. Young people also hear conflicting information from parents, friends, teachers, and acquaintances. Often, they will hear only one side of an issue or be given flawed information. People who are trying to support a particular viewpoint may cite inaccurate facts and statistics on their blogs, and news programs present many conflicting views of important issues in our society. In a world where it seems everyone has a platform to share their thoughts, it can be difficult to find unbiased, accurate information about important issues.

It is not only facts that are important. In blog posts, in comments on online videos, and on talk shows, people will share opinions that are not necessarily true or false, but can still have a strong impact. For example, many young people struggle with their body image. Seeing or hearing negative comments about particular body types online can have a huge effect on the way someone views himself or herself and may lead to depression and anxiety. Although it is important not to keep information hidden from young people under the guise of protecting them, it is equally important to offer encouragement on issues that affect their mental health.

The titles in the Hot Topics series provide readers with different viewpoints on important issues in today's society. Many of these issues, such as teen pregnancy and Internet safety, are of immediate concern to young people. This series aims to give readers factual context on these crucial topics in a way that lets them form their own opinions. The facts presented throughout also serve to empower readers to help themselves or support people they know who are struggling with many of the challenges adolescents face today. Although negative viewpoints are not ignored or downplayed, this series allows young people to see that the challenges they face are not insurmountable. Eating disorders can be overcome, the Internet can be navigated safely, and pregnant teens do not have to feel hopeless.

Quotes encompassing all viewpoints are presented and cited so readers can trace them back to their original source, verifying for themselves whether the information comes from a reputable place. Additional books and websites are listed, giving readers a starting point from which to continue their own research. Chapter questions encourage discussion, allowing young people to hear and understand their classmates' points of view as they further solidify their own. Full-color photographs and enlightening charts provide a deeper understanding of the topics at hand. All of these features augment the informative text, helping young people understand the world they live in and formulate their own opinions concerning the best way they can improve it.

An American Epidemic.

The health care system in the United States has often been called the most complex in the world. It develops and implements the newest medical technologies, boasts world-class facilities and highly trained doctors, and is capable of providing prompt and cutting-edge patient care. The United States also spends more than any other country on health care, both per capita (per person) and in terms of total health expenditures as a percentage of the gross domestic product (GDP)—the country's total economic output. However, the United States consistently scores at or near the bottom when its health care system is compared with those in other developed countries on issues such as quality, efficiency, and effectiveness of care. According to every independent study, the United States has one of the highest rates of infant mortality, lowest levels of life expectancy, and largest numbers of people without health insurance coverage among developed nations. As Steffie Woolhandler, a professor of medicine at Harvard Medical School and cofounder of Physicians for a National Health Program, put it, "The U.S. has ... arguably the worst [health care system] in the developed world."[1]

In other developed countries, almost everyone is covered by health insurance, typically under some type of government-regulated or government-run program. In the United States, however, health insurance is largely an employer-based, privately operated system. This system has historically had high numbers of uninsured people, leading to repeated attempts at health care reform over the years.

Health Care Affordability

The main reason for the lack of insurance, many experts say, has been affordability; health insurance costs have been rising rapidly since the 1960s. Many Americans want good health insurance but cannot afford it. Many people have access to health insurance through their employers as part of their salary package, but rising costs have caused some employers to drop or cut back on health insurance in recent years. That has left uncovered employees, along with the self-employed, to fend for themselves in the individual insurance policy market, where they historically had little negotiating power and faced large premiums, or monthly payments. In fact, even those who were able to afford insurance may not have been granted coverage by insurers due to preexisting medical conditions—that is, conditions diagnosed before patients applied for insurance. Many others—some estimates say 25 million—purchased policies but were still considered underinsured. This means that in the case of a serious medical event, their insurance would pay for only part of their health expenses, not only because of large co-pays (what the patient pays in addition to insurance) and deductibles (what the patient must pay before the insurance company pays), but also because of annual or lifetime limits in their policies. Counting both the uninsured and the underinsured, Jonathan Cohn, author of *Sick: The Untold Story of America's Health Care Crisis—And the People Who Pay the Price*, estimated in 2008 that "almost one fourth of Americans don't have adequate health benefits."[2]

According to health experts, this lack of adequate health insurance has had far-reaching consequences for families, communities, and U.S. society. According to the Health and Medicine Division (HMD)—formerly the Institute of Medicine (IOM)—an independent health research group in the National Academy of Sciences, people without health insurance experience poorer health, die sooner, and are more likely to go bankrupt as a result of health costs than those who are insured—all tragic results for them and their loved ones. Having a large number of uninsured citizens also reduces the financial stability of local hospitals and medical providers, decreasing access and quality of care for everyone in the community. According to many researchers, societal costs are incurred as well, in terms of reduced work productivity, taxpayer dollars spent on emergency and government-subsidized care, and loss of public confidence in American ideals of fairness and equality.

The Affordable Care Act

In March 2010, the U.S. Congress passed the Patient Protection and Affordable Care Act (PPACA or ACA), a landmark health care reform law championed by President Barack Obama, drastically reducing the number of uninsured people in the United States. According to a September 2009 report from the U.S. Census Bureau, pre-ACA passage, 46.3 million Americans, or roughly 15 percent of the total population, had no health insurance in 2008. By 2016, according to a study by the Centers for Disease Control and Prevention (CDC), that number had fallen to 28.2 million Americans under age 65. However, that number has been on the rise since then.

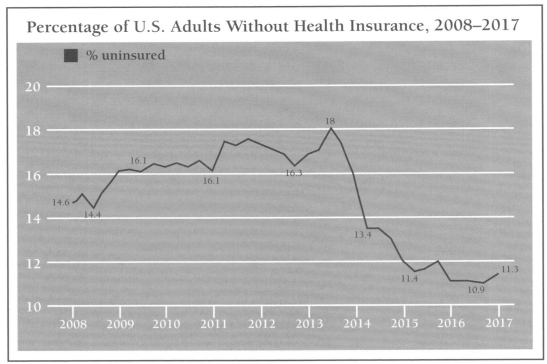

Percentage of U.S. Adults Without Health Insurance, 2008–2017

The number of American adults without health insurance dropped dramatically after 2013, as this information from Gallup shows. This is because in 2014, the Affordable Care Act started requiring uninsured people to pay a penalty.

Although record numbers of Americans now have access to health insurance, many other problems have arisen, leading to more recent reform attempts. Health insurance premiums have risen significantly. Additionally, premiums for plans sold under the ACA were projected to increase dramatically in 2018, making them unaffordable for many people. A study by Avalere Health, a prominent health care consulting firm based in Washington, D.C., showed that deductibles have risen as well, up 17 percent on average. In addition, there are fewer plans available in the ACA marketplace, leading to reduced competition and increased prices as insurance companies continue to withdraw. According to Avalere, seven states currently have only one participating insurance provider for all counties, which means that even if customers are unhappy with their insurance provider, they are unable to switch to a competitor.

In addition to increasing costs and decreasing competition among health care plans for consumers, states have seen an increase in the cost of the Medicaid expansion aspect included in the ACA due to higher than expected enrollment numbers for Medicaid, which is government-funded health care for low-income people. The Foundation for Government Accountability, a Florida-based free market think tank, tracked data for 24 states and found that in those states, 11.5 million people enrolled in Medicaid, significantly up from the 5.5 million projected.

As of early 2018, the ACA is the latest major health care reform attempt that has been passed, and there have been major improvements as well as challenges to the health care industry in the United States since its passage in 2010. Government agencies are hard at work trying to come up with solutions to these challenges while preserving the benefits. However, health care reform has a very long historical precedent of failures and false starts that far outnumber the relative successes, so there is a long, difficult road still ahead to come up with something that works for everyone.

CHAPTER 1

Understanding Health Care

The system of medical care most people are familiar with, in which they pay health insurance providers to pay a person's medical costs on their behalf, is actually a relatively new phenomenon in what is now the United States. During colonial times, medicine was largely a highly unscientific guessing game. Medical practitioners used to believe that the body contained four "humors" that corresponded to the four elements—blood (fire), phlegm (earth), black bile (water), and yellow bile (air)—and that the work of physicians was to maintain a balance among these influences. In service of this view, many early medical treatments involved somehow removing some of these humors from the body to restore them to a proper balance, which they believed would cure whatever ailments someone might have. Medical treatments included bleedings (withdrawing sometimes considerable amounts of blood from sick patients) and purgings (using laxatives or other types of medicines to make patients vomit or otherwise excrete wastes). None of these treatments were particularly effective, and in fact, most were actively harmful. Medical schools were still many years away, and medical training largely consisted of apprenticing with a current practitioner and doing what they did. Medicines were mainly made of various herbs and chemicals, which could often be toxic to the patient as there was almost no scientific basis to any of this. If someone was unfortunate enough to fall ill during the era in which these practices were what passed for medicine, they typically paid for their own treatment—assuming they survived it. Costs were generally quite low, likely due to the fact that there was no expensive equipment and patients stood roughly an equal chance of dying as they did of being cured.

During the second half of the 19th century, however, advances in biology and chemistry helped medical doctors better understand the human body, incorporating principles of modern science into the practice of medicine. Sanitation became an important method of preventing infection, more effective treatments for diseases and injuries were developed, and surgical techniques were refined. In 1847, the American Medical Association (AMA) was founded to create professional standards for doctors and set minimum educational requirements. Thereafter, numerous medical colleges were established, medical research expanded, and

Nathan Smith Davis was one of the founders of the American Medical Association (AMA).

hospitals were built across the nation. During the 20th century, the state of medical care and technologies developed even more. However, as medicine became more effective, the cost of care rose, and a system of health insurance gradually developed to help people pay for this more advanced health care.

The Beginning of Heath Insurance

According to Cohn, the modern era of medicine in the United States began in the 1920s. Around this time, the cost of medical care had exploded to the point that it became unaffordable to many Americans. When the United States and world economies began to sink into the Great Depression in the late 1920s, the situation only worsened. As Cohn explained, "The average cost of a week in the hospital began to exceed what the majority of Americans earned in a month, making illness a scary financial proposition for even the thriftiest middle-class households—and forcing many people to skip medical care altogether."[3]

To address this problem, several private charitable founda-
tions established the Committee on the Costs of Medical Care
(CCMC) in 1927 to study the health care crisis and report on
possible solutions. The committee's final report in October 1932
recommended the creation of health insurance for medical care.
The report explained that this made sense because health expenses tend to be concentrated on people with serious medical
conditions, and since everyone faced the prospect of some type
of serious medical crisis during their lifetime, health costs could
be reduced if collective systems were developed to insure against
serious illness.

One of the first efforts to provide prepaid health care was
initiated by Baylor Hospital in Dallas, Texas, in 1929, even
before the CCMC's report was released. The hospital's admin-
istrator, Justin Ford Kimball, who had a background working
with public schools, offered to provide up to two weeks of
hospital care for local teachers if at least three-quarters of the
teachers in the region agreed to be part of the plan. The Baylor
plan worked, covering the hospital costs of about 1,500 teachers
for a monthly premium of about 50 cents. This helped both the
teachers and the hospital, which was in debt because people
were not paying their bills. News of the success of this early
insurance plan spread around the country to other hospitals and
eventually evolved into a national system called Blue Cross.

The early Blue Cross insurers were typically private nonprofit organizations created to cover large groups of people,
such as the employees of a company, because they needed a
pool large enough to spread the risks. Even though they were
private entities, these early insurers provided a public benefit.
They charged everyone the same premium regardless of age,
sex, or preexisting conditions—a system called community
rate—and many also provided some form of insurance to individuals not associated with any group, as long as they agreed
to pay their premiums. With no pressure to produce profits,
premiums were kept low, supported only by government tax
deductions. As Cohn explained, Blue Cross thus "resemble[d]
social insurance—a protection scheme in which healthy people
subsidized the costs of the sick, precisely as the Committee on

the Cost of Medicine had recommended in 1932."[4] Some people opposed health insurance because they thought it sounded too much like socialism, a system of government in which the government owns everything and determines what citizens get. This view has persisted in some forms throughout the years and is often brought up in the health care debate. However, in the 1920s, these fears were outweighed by the desire for affordable health care.

AN UNINTENDED CONSEQUENCE

"In practice, Kimball's approach meant health insurance paid the hospital bill, no matter how high the charges. That made health insurance an ally of providers rather than patients, helping to push up the cost of care. It set health insurance in a direction that took 50 years to change."
—Jim Landers, journalist, on the creation of health insurance

Jim Landers, "Since Insurance's Humble Start in Dallas, Hospital Inflation Has Always Posed Challenge," Dallas News, March 2015. www.dallasnews.com/business/business/2015/03/06/since-insurance-s-humble-start-in-dallas-hospital-inflation-has-always-posed-challenge.

Health Insurance as a Benefit

The entrance of America into World War II in the 1940s helped establish a uniquely American system of employer-based health insurance. When the government imposed wage controls on employers during the war, many employers began offering health insurance as an employee benefit. The United States at that time suffered from a very tight labor market, since many workers were in active duty with the armed forces, and health insurance was one of the few incentives employers could offer to attract qualified employees. The federal government encouraged this trend by offering employers tax deductions for health care expenses and allowing the insurance benefit to be tax-free to employees. The National Labor Relations Board also ruled that health benefits could be part of collective bargaining agreements, so unions supported the employer-based system as well.

After World War II ended in 1945, employers continued to offer health insurance because it had become such a popular job benefit. As a result, this model of health insurance expanded to cover more and more workers. The benefits offered under these plans expanded as well, giving people more medical services and improvements in medical technologies. In these early postwar years, the primary insurance provider was Blue Cross. Because Blue Cross initially provided coverage only for hospital services, Blue Shield plans were created to cover doctor services

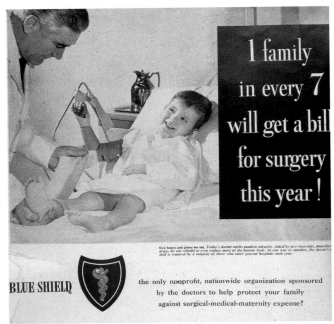

such as yearly checkups, and the name became Blue Cross Blue Shield (BCBS). According to some estimates, more than 20 million Americans had enrolled in BCBS plans by 1950, providing widespread coverage for many working people. Of course, the costs of the insurance rose along with improvements in care, but during the postwar period, the U.S. economy was booming and employers were willing to absorb the extra costs.

By the end of the 1950s, commercial insurance companies had replaced the original nonprofit health insurance model with a for-profit model.

Health Insurance as a Business Plan

The success of the early BCBS plans, in turn, encouraged private commercial insurers to begin offering health insurance, and by the end of the 1950s, prominent insurance companies such as Prudential, Aetna, and Metropolitan Life of New York had entered the field. The presence of these commercial companies, however, fundamentally changed the BCBS model of health insurance, which sought to cover everyone. According to many health care experts, the root of this transformation was that commercial insurers were not as concerned with serving the public good; as private companies, their goal was to make money. Therefore, unlike BCBS—which charged everyone the same premium, in effect requiring healthy people to subsidize the sick—commercial insurers sought to attract healthy people by offering them cheaper policies that more closely reflected their individual health risks. Rates were then adjusted when subscribers' health status changed. The elderly and those who were already sick, who seemed to pose the highest risk for insurers, were charged much higher rates and sometimes rejected for coverage altogether.

This strategy, known as experience rating, permitted the commercial insurers to substantially undercut the premiums offered to healthy people by BCBS. Within just a few years, enrollment in commercial insurance plans exceeded the number of people insured by BCBS. Ultimately, the competition forced BCBS insurers to adopt the same experience rating model used by commercial insurance firms, and the nonprofit community rate system completely disappeared. It simply could not survive after the youngest, healthiest people were signed up by commercial insurers.

The end of the community rate system was finally confirmed in 1986, when Congress officially removed the tax breaks historically provided to BCBS, after a finding by the U.S. Internal Revenue Service (IRS) that the company was no longer any different from commercial insurers.

The effect of the privatization—control of the market by private companies that operate for profit—of health insurance on the access of Americans to quality, affordable health care was dramatic. As for-profit insurers focused on insuring people in good health, sicker and older Americans found it increasingly difficult to find affordable health insurance. As this higher-risk population was peeled away from the broader community of mostly healthy people, the costs of insuring them grew significantly. Also, since health insurance in the United States was largely employer-based, only people employed by large companies even stood a chance of being offered affordable health insurance coverage. The unemployed (which included large numbers of retired elderly), the self-employed, and people employed at small businesses faced the highest costs because, unlike the numerous employees of a large company, they did not have access to a large insurance pool in which risk could be spread to keep down premium costs. In fact, even when healthy individuals were willing to pay extremely high premiums, many insurers simply refused to provide policies, sometimes on controversial grounds such as race, sex, age, or occupation, which insurers defended as relevant to the amount and cost of health care the patient might use. Many health care experts therefore conclude that the privatization of health care led to higher health care costs and created a larger uninsured population in the United States. As Harvard Medical School professor Arnold S. Relman argued,

> Markets are not concerned with justice or equity. When private health care and insurance are sold in commercial markets by profit-driven providers, access is limited largely to those who can afford to pay—or those whose employers pay for them ... There can be little doubt that the swelling army of uninsured and underinsured, and the progressive fraying of coverage, are the result of high costs in our market-driven system.[5]

IS IT WORTH IT?

"While it's true that we're paying 14 times as many dollars for health care as we did in 1950, we're getting an amazing return on our investment. Since 1950, the average U.S. life expectancy has increased by almost nine years."
—Sally C. Pipes, president and CEO of the Pacific Research Institute, a conservative think tank that promotes free market principles

Sally C. Pipes, The Top Ten Myths of American Health Care: A Citizen's Guide. San Francisco, CA: Pacific Research Institute, 2008, p. 25.

Important Terms

Health insurance has its own vocabulary that can often be confusing. Below are some of the most commonly used terms.

cap: A limit on the services insurers provide. For example, the number of visits to a specialist may be capped at four per year, although the actual number varies depending on the plan. After that point, the patient must pay out of pocket.

co-pay: An amount paid each time a medical service is accessed. For instance, a health insurance plan may cover most of the cost of a doctor's visit, but the patient is often responsible for paying a small amount at the time of the visit. This varies from plan to plan; some plans have no co-pay, while others may charge upwards of $30. Co-pays do not count toward a deductible.

deductible: An amount that must be paid before insurance will start covering costs. For instance, someone whose plan includes a $500 deductible would have to pay $500 out of pocket on doctors, medication, and other health care costs before their insurance starts covering their expenses. Generally, the lower the premium, the higher the deductible. Deductibles reset every year.

out-of-pocket costs: Costs paid by the patient that are not covered by insurance. Co-pays and deductibles are examples of out-of-pocket costs. Under the ACA, a patient's out-of-pocket costs are capped, so the patient is no longer responsible for medical costs after a certain threshold is reached; for example, individuals do not have to pay more than $7,150.

premium: A monthly fee paid to the insurance company, which funds the insurance. Generally, the higher the premium, the more the plan covers.

The Introduction of Medicare and Medicaid

Another historic change in the American health care system came in 1965, when Medicare was created to help elderly people deal with the rising costs of health care in the new private insurance markets, as they often lived on a post-retirement fixed income. As of 1965, only about half of all seniors were covered by a health insurance plan. As people age, they typically face more frequent, more serious health issues. As a result, many seniors faced huge medical bills that they could not pay—bills that caused terrible financial hardship and were a leading cause of poverty among the elderly during this period.

President John F. Kennedy campaigned for a broad government plan to help the elderly in 1960, and after Kennedy's assassination in November 1963, the country's new president, Lyndon Baines Johnson, took up the cause of senior health care. During this period, a growing U.S. economy helped create widespread public support for the idea of taking care of the health of older people. Congress finally acted on the issue after Johnson was elected president by a landslide in 1964, and the president signed the landmark Medicare program into law on July 30, 1965. The original Medicare program had three parts: Medicare Part A, which paid for most hospital care, skilled nursing care for a limited time, and some home health care for all elderly Americans; Medicare Part B, which paid for visits to the doctor as long as seniors opted for the program and paid premiums; and Medicaid, a separate program, which paid for health care for people who were receiving welfare benefits. As former senator Tom Daschle noted, "The final Medicare bill represented the largest expansion of health-care coverage in American history."[6]

President Lyndon B. Johnson signed the Medicare Bill into law on July 30, 1965.

Medicare and Medicaid were a tremendous help to elderly, disabled, and very poor Americans, providing them with the health care safety net they so desperately needed. As health care expert Marian E. Gornick explained in a 1996 article about Medicare's 30th anniversary, "With the implementation of Medicare on July 1, 1966, virtually the entire elderly population in the Nation was made eligible for Part A coverage, and almost all had voluntarily enrolled in Part B."[7] The out-of-pocket medical costs for these groups were significantly reduced as a direct result of the legislation. In addition, mortality rates for seniors decreased over the next few decades, and many health experts credit these declining death rates among elderly people at least in part to the increased access to medical care provided by Medicare and Medicaid.

By removing some of the highest-risk beneficiaries—what health insurance companies call their customers—from the overall pool of people needing health care and providing them with government-paid health care, the Medicare program also took the pressure off private insurers and, in this way, strengthened the private health care insurance system. However, most experts in the health field also say that Medicare helped to increase health care costs even more; because the government was paying for care, hospitals could charge more, knowing their bills would be paid. It also created an overreliance on hospitals, according to economics website The Balance. Rather than going to their regular doctor or waiting to see if their illness resolved itself, many people headed straight for a hospital as soon as they got sick, increasing the number of patients, emergency room wait times, and expenses. Emergency room visits cost much more than a regular doctor visit, so this also increased Medicare spending.

Medicaid has also been controversial, with people opposing it because it covers those who cannot afford to pay into an insurance program. In some people's view, this is unfair to those who can pay. Others disagree, saying that it is a society's duty to provide assistance for people who are living below the poverty line (the minimum income level needed to acquire the basic necessities for living). In 2011, the *New York Times* reported on a study that found providing health insurance to people who could not afford it had many benefits; for example, "they not only find regular doctors and see doctors more often but they also feel better, are less depressed and are better able to maintain financial stability."[8] However, for years, funding for Medicare and Medicaid has been debated, and this debate will likely continue in the future.

HEALTH CARE IS A BUSINESS

"Health care is the largest industry in the United States, employing more than 14 million people. Health care expenditures totaled over $2.5 trillion—17.9% of the entire US economy— in 2011."
—ProCon.org, a nonprofit organization devoted to promoting critical thinking

"ProCon.org Publishes New Nonpartisan Review of 'Obamacare,'" ProCon.org, October 16, 2012. www.procon.org/headline.php?headlineID=005126.

Increasing Costs and the Rise of Managed Care

The soaring health care costs in the 1960s, 1970s, and 1980s led to efforts to control costs through managed care—a term that generally refers to health insurance plans that seek to exercise control over the quantity and quality of health care services provided to beneficiaries rather than simply pay the bills submitted by medical providers. Employers were at the forefront of the push for managed care because they had experienced decades of unpredictable and uncontrolled premium increases for their employees, only part of which employers could ask employees to pay. The managed care plans generally offered much cheaper premium rates to employers and beneficiaries than typical health insurance plans.

One of the first types of low-cost managed care plans was developed in the early 1970s and was called the health maintenance organization (HMO). The first HMOs, like the early Blue Cross plans, were nonprofits that sought to emphasize preventive care, which would lead to lower medical costs down

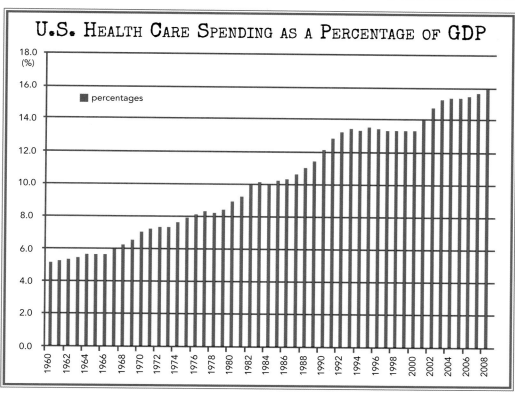

American spending on health care has more than doubled since 1960, as this information from the Organisation for Economic Co-operation and Development (OECD) shows.

the line by catching health problems before they needed major treatment. Additionally, they tried to provide health care at a lower cost by restricting beneficiaries to a network of medical providers who agreed to various rules geared toward reducing costs. This means people with HMO insurance cannot go just anywhere if they want insurance to cover it; they must see someone in their network (out-of-network providers will not accept their insurance). This is often not a problem when it comes to individual doctors, as networks are typically large and include many doctors specializing in all kinds of medicine. However, they may find that the closest clinic or hospital is not in their network, which can be a problem in an emergency or when someone gets sick on vacation. As insurance expert Corinne Mitchell explained,

When HMO Plans were first introduced, members paid a fixed, pre-paid monthly premium in exchange for health care from a contracted network of providers. The contracted network of providers includes hospitals, clinics and health care providers that have signed a contract with the HMO. In this sense, HMOs are the most restrictive form of managed care plans because they restrict the procedures, providers and benefits by requiring that the members use these providers and no others.[9]

The federal government also subsidized HMOs—paid for part of them to reduce the cost for individuals—helping them to grow. In 1973, President Richard Nixon signed the Health Maintenance Organization Act—a law that gave millions of dollars in grants and loans to HMOs and provided incentives for employers to offer them as an option along with traditional health insurance plans. By the mid-1990s, more insured Americans were enrolled in HMOs than in traditional health care plans.

Shown here is Caspar Weinberger, Secretary of Health, Education and Welfare in 1973, explaining the details of the Health Maintenance Organization Act.

The HMO plans were successful for a while at holding down health care costs, but over time, most HMOs became more and more restrictive. They frequently imposed difficult conditions on doctors, such as requiring them to see more patients and get preapproval from the insurance company before providing many types of medical services. The HMOs also began to deny

Choosing a Plan

Choosing an insurance plan can be confusing and frustrating, and it often feels a lot like gambling. There are many different variables to consider; people have to ask themselves questions such as, "How often do I get sick? How likely am I to have a large medical expense soon? What can I afford? Do I need mental health care, and does this plan cover it?" Someone who does not get sick often or does not have a lot of money to spend may opt for a high-deductible, low-premium plan, where they pay more each time they go to the doctor but have a lower monthly fee. However, if something unexpected happens—if they discover they have a disease such as cancer, for instance, or they are in a car accident—they may find themselves paying a lot more than they bargained for. Some employers help people with high-deductible plans by adding to their health savings account (HSA), which is money people can save and spend on medical expenses without paying taxes on it. *TIME* magazine offered this advice:

> *Choosing a plan your doctor accepts is a must. From there, if you're relatively healthy and you have enough savings to cover a health care emergency, a high-deductible plan often makes sense, especially if your employer adds cash to your HSA. But if you tend to have high health care costs, you're short on savings, or your employer isn't adding to your HSA as an incentive, take a careful look at your potential outlay—it may be worth paying more upfront for better coverage later.*[1]

1. Kara Brandeisky, "How to Pick a Health Plan in 15 Minutes or Less," *TIME*, October 19, 2015. time.com/money/4066464/choose-health-insurance/.

many claims for medical care submitted by beneficiaries, claiming they were too expensive or unnecessary. Some commentators suggest the reason for this is that the HMO industry, like the early traditional health insurers, had become by this time a for-profit endeavor that saw profits in the new restrictions. As a result, however, HMOs have become much less popular than they once were, as well as less affordable.

As HMOs declined, insurers began to promote another form of managed care—preferred provider organization (PPO) insurance. Under PPO plans, subscribers select physicians from a group of doctors who have agreed to be preferred providers for that insurance company, but patients are still free to consult specialists (from a list of preferred providers) without a referral from their primary doctor. A referral is essentially a permission slip; when a specialist requires a referral, the patient's primary doctor must approve their patient's visit. Theoretically, insurance companies can control costs through these plans by getting preferred providers to agree to being paid a certain amount by the insurance company. However, largely because patients can visit specialists—who are more expensive—whenever they want, the cost of medical care under PPOs has become more expensive than under the HMO model.

The Road to Reform

Health care costs continued to skyrocket in the late 1990s and early 2000s, pressuring employers and causing many, especially smaller, companies to reduce or completely eliminate health care benefits for employees. Other employers struggled to maintain health insurance but changed to policies with higher deductibles or policies that required employees to cover more of the cost. Premiums for individual health insurance policies also rose greatly, making health insurance often completely unaffordable for many self-employed or unemployed individuals, as well as for the ever-growing number of working people not covered by an employer policy. People who were sick or had preexisting conditions—broadly interpreted by health insurance companies to mean any evidence of a health problem prior to signing up for a health insurance policy—often found it impossible to find coverage at any cost. Because so many Americans were underinsured or without coverage, most health experts agreed that America was once again facing a health care crisis. This crisis prompted repeated attempts at reform and spurred a national health care debate, leading to the writing and 2010 passage of landmark legislation, the Patient Protection and Affordable Care Act (PPACA or ACA), which has been the law ever since.

The Challenges of Health Care Reform

As medical advances continued and some form of health insurance increasingly became the norm, costs of health care–related expenses continued to rise. There have been nearly constant debates and attempts to reform health care over the past 100 years, with many people working to provide affordable and accessible health care for all Americans. This has been a difficult goal to achieve, as multiple presidents—from Franklin Delano Roosevelt onward—and multiple sessions of Congress have found their efforts blocked due to opposition from various quarters, from the AMA to lobbyists for the private health insurance industry, who have consistently been able to portray any reform attempts at expanding medical coverage as "socialism." The United States has long had a strongly negative reaction toward anything socialized due to various global and historical factors, and any meaningful reform has been exceptionally difficult to push through the legislative process. A landmark piece of health care legislation, the ACA, was finally passed in 2010, but insurance costs for the average American continue to rise despite this effort. The health care debate remains as controversial as ever, with different political parties having very different ultimate goals in mind, and it is likely to continue for many years to come.

A Century of Futility

One of the very first health care reform efforts was made by the American Association of Labor Legislation (AALL), an organization of reformers active during the early part of the 20th century. The group's 1915 model health care bill proposed comprehensive national health insurance coverage for the working class and the poor, with program costs shared among workers, employers, and the state. This model was hotly debated and introduced as legislation in several states, but it eventually failed due to opposition from three highly influential groups—the AMA, the American Federation of Labor, and commercial insurers. America's entry into World War I against Germany in 1917 sealed the fate of the AALL bill, as anti-German sentiment grew in America and opponents of health care reform associated it with German socialism.

The idea of national health insurance arose again in the 1930s, after America sank into the Great Depression—a worldwide economic slowdown in which millions of Americans lost their jobs, their homes, and their money. Faced with this unprecedented challenge, Roosevelt created the Committee on Economic Security to study the problems of economic insecurity and offer solutions as part of his New Deal legislative platform. The committee studied four types of social insurance—unemployment insurance, public employment and relief, old age security, and medical care—and it included a national health care plan in its report to the president. However, in the face of AMA opposition that was based on doctors' fears that they would lose money or have to do what the government told them to, Roosevelt decided not to push for health insurance to be part of the legislative social security bill that was working its way through Congress, for fear that it would ruin his chances to get other important programs enacted. As a result, Roosevelt's 1935 Social Security Act—which set up a broad program of old age, disability, and unemployment insurance—did not include any type of national health insurance. Because of the Depression, unemployment and old age benefits ranked higher on the president's list of national priorities.

A later proposal for national health care introduced to Congress by New York Senator Robert F. Wagner met the same fate, and Roosevelt died in April 1945 without offering another health insurance proposal. When World War II started, national health insurance again got pushed aside in favor of more pressing concerns.

When World War II ended in 1945, the next U.S. president, Harry Truman, also came out strongly in favor of a universal, comprehensive national health insurance plan. However,

The Social Security Act of 1935, signed by President Franklin D. Roosevelt, included old age pensions and unemployment insurance but failed to include health care provisions.

Truman's reform efforts ultimately failed, like earlier reforms, due to strong opposition from the AMA and its allies, who called Truman's bill "socialized medicine" because it would involve too much government control. Anti-communist sentiment was widespread throughout this Cold War era—the period following World War II when the United States and Russia maintained an openly hostile relationship due to differing political ideologies—and Russian communism, like socialism, was an ideology in which the government exerted control over most or all parts of the economy.

In fact, the first major U.S. health care reform did not happen until 20 years later, when Johnson created Medicare and Medicaid in 1965. This milestone law finally achieved some of the health care goals sought by Roosevelt and Truman. The signing ceremony for the new law was even held in Independence,

Missouri, Truman's hometown, so he could attend. However, Medicare and Medicaid only provided health care insurance for the old, the disabled, and the poor; many working-class and middle-class families who did not have health insurance through employers were still left without affordable health insurance.

The first modern push for reform to provide universal health insurance for all Americans occurred in 1971, when various people were campaigning to be their party's presidential candidate in the 1972 presidential election. Republican President Richard Nixon supported a market-based approach that continued America's employer-based system of health insurance, while Democratic Senator Edward Kennedy supported a government-run program similar to Medicare. After Nixon was reelected president, he introduced his Comprehensive Health Insurance Act—a bill that required employers to purchase health insurance for employees but also set up a federal health plan available to Americans on a sliding scale based on income. However, when Nixon became involved in a political scandal known as Watergate, support for him and his programs decreased dramatically, and the bill was never passed.

Despite rising health care costs, neither of the next two presidents—Republican Gerald Ford and Democrat Jimmy Carter—were able to make headway on health care reforms. President Ronald Reagan tried to enact the 1988 Medicare Catastrophic Coverage Act (MCCA)—the biggest expansion of Medicare since its creation in 1965—but since it was funded by charging wealthier Medicare recipients an extra tax, many people did not like it. Because of this opposition, Congress decided to repeal the law just one year later.

Following the MCCA failure, it was not until President Bill Clinton took office in 1993 that health care reform once again became part of the national agenda. Clinton set up a task force on the issue headed by then–First Lady Hillary Clinton. The Clinton proposal, called the Health Security Act, required that all Americans be covered by health insurance either through their employers or through government-run regional alliances, with competition among insurers regulated by the government. However, like other attempts to create universal health insurance, the bill was attacked for allowing too much government control over health care. Ultimately, the Clinton bill was defeated by a media campaign created by the insurance industry. The campaign was called "Harry and Louise" and featured ordinary Americans criticizing the bill as too complex and bureaucratic. The defeat of the Clinton health care reform package largely pushed the issue to the political sidelines until the 2008 presidential election.

As First Lady, Hillary Clinton met with seniors as part of the information campaign for the ultimately doomed Health Security Act.

Health Care as a Partisan Issue

The political debate about how to solve the health care crisis continued to be highly partisan—split largely along party lines—with few areas of agreement. Views differed even on the most basic question of whether health care reform was needed. Many Republicans and other conservatives believed, for example, that the free market system of health care and health care insurance in the United States provided the best health care in the world. As Republican President George W. Bush said in a 2004 presidential debate, "Our health care system is the envy of the world."[10] Conservatives pointed out that people from other nations often came to the United States for medical care because America offered such cutting-edge treatments and technologies. Karl Rove, former deputy chief of staff to Bush, noted some of these accomplishments:

> From 1998 to 2002 nearly twice as many new drugs were launched in the U.S. as in Europe. According to the U.S. Pharmaceutical Industry Report, some 2,900 new drugs are now being researched here. America's five top hospitals conduct more clinical trials than all the hospitals in any other developed country.[11]

As a result, many on the political right argued that the existing system of private health insurance and medical care was not broken and should not be fundamentally changed. As Rove stated, "[The] trashing of American health care as 'a broken system' ... doesn't resonate with most Americans. They are happy about their health care, doctor and hospital. [A 2009] ... poll found that 83% of Americans are very or somewhat satisfied with the quality of care they and their families receive."[12] However, a 2016 poll conducted by National Public Radio (NPR), the Robert Wood Johnson Foundation, and the Harvard T. H. Chan School of Public Health showed that while "80 percent [of people] say they get good or excellent care ... 42 percent rate the health care system in their state as fair or poor."[13] In other words, while people may feel their own doctor provides good care, they do not like the health care system as a whole. Often this is because of the paperwork, expenses, being ordered to take the same lab tests multiple times for the same condition, and having to make visits to multiple doctors or multiple visits to the same doctor to get an accurate diagnosis. According to Sarah Dash, vice president for health policy at the Alliance for Health Policy in Washington, D.C., "Health care hasn't always been designed with the needs and efficiency of the patient in mind ... It's designed for the various doctors and the health care system."[14]

The Health Care Debate in Pop Culture

Few movies and TV shows discuss the details of health care reform because most Americans do not consider it an interesting topic. When it is discussed in pop culture, it generally focuses on people who are fighting the system. For instance, in the movie *John Q.*, a man takes several people hostage in a hospital emergency room until his son is given a heart transplant, which the family cannot afford to pay for and their insurance refuses to cover.

However, one TV show that tackles this topic is *Superstore*, a comedy about people who work in a store similar to Wal-Mart. In the episode "Health Fund," one employee gets an ear infection but cannot afford to treat it because the store's insurance plan does not cover much. The employees try to start a health fund in which everyone contributes a certain amount of money, but they quickly find out that some of their coworkers need more medical care than others. The situation spirals out of control, and the plan gets unmanageable. One employee voices the opinion of many people who are unaware of how complex health insurance is: "We just gotta simplify. Cover everything, exclude no one, and make it affordable."[1] However, over the course of the episode, they realize this is easier said than done. Eventually, another employee sums up the key problem with health insurance reform: "Some of us are gonna use the fund more than others, but no one wants to put in more money than they're going to take out."[2] With such a complicated problem to solve, it is understandable that health care reform in the United States will continue to require experts to put in time and effort.

1. Quoted in Antonia Le, "Superstore—Health Fund—Review: 'You Solved Healthcare!,'" Spoiler TV, November 5, 2017. www.spoilertv.com/2017/11/superstore-health-fund-review-you.html.
2. Quoted in Le, "Superstore—Health Fund."

The results of this poll also showed that satisfaction with health care was largely dependent on how much money a person has. Most liberals have argued for years that the American health care system only provides good health care for the rich, leaving increasingly large portions of the population without access to affordable health care or health insurance. They cited a 1986 report by the Institute of Medicine (IOM), which found significant deficiencies and variations in the quality of U.S. medical care. Similarly, a review of the world's health care systems in 2000 by the World Health Organization (WHO), a United Nations (UN) health agency, ranked the United States behind nearly every other industrialized country in terms of the quality of its medical care, most especially in promoting the same quality of care for everyone. In December 2017, Professor Philip Alston, a representative of the UN, visited the United States to investigate poverty in certain states. His report noted several important facts:

- *US health care expenditures per capita [per person] are ... much higher than in all other countries. But there are many fewer doctors and hospital beds per person ...*

- *US infant mortality rates in 2013 were the highest in the developed world.*

- *Americans can expect to live shorter and sicker lives, compared to people living in any other rich democracy, and the "health gap" between the U.S. and its peer countries continues to grow.*[15]

As Daschle argued, "At the dawn of the twenty-first century, we are the only industrialized nation that does not guarantee necessary health care to all of its citizens. It is stunning and shameful."[16]

Quality and Income

Poll: "Overall, how would you rate the health care you receive?"

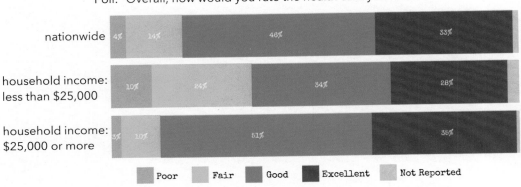

Families who live in poverty are less likely to be satisfied with the quality of the health care they receive, as this information from NPR shows.

According to a 2009 IOM report, uninsured Americans tended to go without health care and were therefore more likely to suffer from unnecessary illness, greater limitations in quality of life, and premature death. According to a study published in the *American Journal of Public Health* in 2009, nearly 45,000 Americans die annually from lack of health insurance. Not having health insurance can also quickly bankrupt a family in the event of a medical emergency. Even people who were insured found that their insurance paid only around 80 percent of major medical bills, so the insured were at risk, too, in the event of serious illness or injury. According to a study published in the *American Journal of Medicine*, "Using a conservative definition, 62.1% of all bankruptcies in 2007 were medical ... Most medical debtors were well educated, owned homes, and had middle class occupations. Three quarters had health insurance."[17] This situation, many experts believe, frays the fabric of civil society as well as the economy, weakening America from the inside.

Medical bills can be very expensive, and trying to pay them can cause people to declare bankruptcy or even lose their home.

NOT DOING ENOUGH

"Despite all the rights and privileges and entitlements that Americans enjoy today, we have never decided to provide medical care for everybody who needs it."
—T. R. Reid, author and journalist

T. R. Reid, The Healing of America: The Global Quest for Better, Cheaper, and Fairer Health Care. New York, NY: Penguin, 2009. p. 2.

How Involved Should the Government Be?

Among those policy makers who agree that the U.S. health care system needs improvement, perhaps the biggest disagreement is over the role of government. The majority of conservatives favor keeping a completely private market system in which not only the medical providers but also health insurers are for-profit companies. Reforming this system, according to conservative analysts, hinges on empowering patients to be intelligent consumers of health care services so they can choose their medical services and insurance and pay a larger share of health care costs.

Conservatives are more likely than liberals to believe that health insurance would benefit from less government involvement. Many argue for a free-market model in which people pay for most of their own health care. The basic idea is that if patients have to pay for their own health care, they will demand a higher quality of care, and the competition for these health consumers will lower health care costs. If two companies are offering the same service and both do an equally good job, people are more likely to choose the one that is cheaper, so competition between companies can encourage companies to keep their prices low. Conservatives point to certain types of health care that are already competitive because they are typically not covered by insurance—such as laser eye surgery—and note that free market competition in these services has led both to quality improvements and to falling prices. In a 2017 debate between conservative John Davidson and liberal Maria Svart, Davidson argued,

As it is, the U.S. health care system disconnects patients from the cost of their care ... Why does a single aspirin cost $25 in a hospital? Why does sinus surgery cost $5,885 in one facility and $33,505 in another?

You can't have a functioning market without clear price signals, and the way we treat health insurance hides prices and divorces us from the cost of care. Think of it this way: if car insurance were like health insurance, premiums wouldn't just cover damage from accidents, they would cover gas, oil changes, tire replacement, windshield wipers, and so on. No one would know what those things cost individually, but premiums would be very high ...

The real cost drivers in health care aren't really insurance companies or [pharmaceutical companies], but the hospital systems that insurers have to have in their networks. Hospitals charge high prices because insurers will pay whatever they ask.[18]

More politically liberal people, however, tend to disagree with the consumer model; they are convinced that the private market will not save the U.S. health care system. Asking people to pay more for health care when they already cannot afford basic care, they say, would only leave more people outside the system. Additionally, some argue that health insurance does not follow the same rules as other free-market services. For instance, when people are shopping for a kitchen appliance or a new car, they can choose not to buy from a store if they do not like the price. When they need health care, however, it is often a matter of life and death; they may not have the option to wait until competition drives the price down. In an emergency situation, such as a car accident, they may not even have a choice at all. They need to get to the nearest hospital, not the cheapest one.

Some people who favor a free-market system have acknowledged the problem of lack of choice in emergency care; for instance, Davidson has proposed that insurance should only cover such emergency situations, the way car insurance only covers accidents. However, others believe this is still not a good enough solution, arguing that in a free market, the quality of the care may suffer. As *Huffington Post* pointed out, "for doctors, patients' interests can often take a back seat to making a buck in a free market health care system—and ... the result can often be poor quality health care at a high cost."[19] Since many people do not have the in-depth medical knowledge a doctor does, it would be difficult for them to tell whether the procedures being ordered are necessary or simply a tactic designed to get them to pay more money. This is also a risk in the current insurance model, but the ones paying for the procedures are the insurance companies rather than the patients. Doctors and pharmaceutical companies would also have an incentive not to provide preventive care because it costs less than curing people after they get sick. In contrast, insurance companies make more money from healthy people than sick ones, so they are more likely to do things that help people avoid disease, such as paying for yearly checkups.

Is Single-Payer the Answer?

Although many do not favor a free-market system, they also acknowledge that the current insurance system is flawed as well. Instead of either model, people who lean toward the more liberal end of the political spectrum tend to favor a government-run health care system. They envision a single-payer government insurance plan paid for by taxes—a plan similar to Medicaid in which all Americans would be covered for basic health care by a government insurance fund, with private doctors and hospitals paid by this fund. During debates, this basic idea has been called by various names—Medicare for All, single-payer, or the public option. The advantages of such a program, supporters say, are many: Only one public insurance agency would be accountable to voters; few or no co-pays, deductibles, or limits on yearly or lifetime costs; no incentive to spend money on advertising or do unethical things to make a profit; small administrative costs; and low, negotiated prices for medications, medical services, and medical equipment. According to many liberals, this type of public health care system would eliminate the private sector profit motive from health care—the central problem in the current system and the key reason for denials of care. As Cynthia Tucker, former editorial page editor for the *Atlanta Journal-Constitution*, explained, "The for-profit health insurance industry is in the business of maximizing profits for their shareholders, and the only way they can do that is to hold down the payments they make for medical care."[20]

Proposals for government-run health plans, however, have always run into a wall of opposition from conservatives, who often equate them with socialism and raise fears about government bureaucracy and a loss of freedom to choose the medical provider they prefer. Some have gone further, worrying that the government would gain too much power and deny people care based on things other than profit. In 2009, soon after Obama proposed the ACA, former vice presidential candidate Sarah Palin claimed the act would allow the government to create "death panels"—meetings in which the government decided whether someone contributed enough to society to be worth receiving life-saving medical care. There was never any evidence that this would happen, and members of the administration repeatedly dismissed the idea; Obama called the claims dishonest, saying "that people who want to keep things the way they are will try to scare the heck out of folks, and they'll create boogeymen out there that just aren't real."[21] Regardless, a distrust for the government as well as a lack of knowledge about what the bill actually contained decreased support for the ACA.

Supporters of the public option point out that truly socialized health care means the government would own all the hospitals and directly employ doctors and other providers—a system far different from Medicaid, in which providers are privately owned and chosen by patients. Of course, a Medicare for All system would take business away from commercial insurance companies—a result that helps explain the industry's historical opposition to government-run reform proposals.

Health Care for All

A major goal of most health reform proposals is universal care—making it available to everyone who needs it, not just those who are healthy or who can afford it. To many experts, basic health care is a human right that all people should have. Others disagree, noting that health care is not guaranteed in the U.S. Constitution. They say health care, like food, shelter, or clothing, is just another type of commodity in the private marketplace and they should not be required to pay for those things for other people. However, many nations, including the United States, provide a government safety net for the poor to provide for basic needs, and Medicaid added health care to this list. Some people argue that a civilized society should offer health care for all Americans as part of this safety net. They believe things that can save someone's life should be provided even if the person cannot afford it.

The health care debate is sharply divided along political lines. Most liberals see it as a right that should be granted to all Americans by the government, while conservatives tend to feel it is a service that should be left to private businesses, with the level of coverage decided upon by the person who buys it.

Part of the problem of extending health care to everyone, however, is that younger, healthier people have less need for health care and may not want to pay for it, either directly or through taxes. When the ACA required everyone to purchase insurance or pay a fine at the end of the year, the backlash from younger people who could not afford to pay for insurance and did not feel they needed it prompted many health insurance companies to begin offering catastrophic health insurance. This type of plan has a very high deductible; it is intended to only cover preventive and emergency health services, and it is only available to people who are under 30 and have a valid reason for not being able to afford regular health insurance. These conditions are in place because a system of universal health care is not possible unless a broad pool of people is insured—the young and healthy help subsidize the sick and, in turn, are covered when they might need medical care. Many health reform proposals, therefore, have included provisions that require individuals or employers to either have health insurance or pay a penalty. Like other parts of reform, however, this compulsory health insurance concept has been controversial, both with small employers and low-income individuals, who say they cannot afford it, and with conservatives, who see it as another government infringement on basic individual freedoms.

Reducing the Cost of Health Care

The most difficult challenge in reforming health care is controlling costs, which rose to $3.2 trillion in 2016, almost $1 trillion more than was spent in 2008. Almost everyone agrees that costs have reached unsustainable levels and are continuing to rise, but there is significant disagreement about both the cause of rising costs and the appropriate solutions. According to an independent health care think tank called the Kaiser Family Foundation, the major drivers of health care costs are new medical technologies and prescription drugs, chronic disease, the aging of the U.S. population, and high administrative costs.

Many health experts on the political left argue that the government-run Medicaid model is more efficient than the private insurance system, pointing out that private insurers have much higher administrative costs. There is support for this argument; according to the Kaiser Family Foundation, "It is estimated that at least 7% of health care expenditures are for [insurers'] administrative costs (e.g., marketing, billing) [but] ... this portion is much lower in the Medicare program (<2%)."[22] In fact, liberals often argue that the privatization of health care and health insurance is the real root of rising costs.

Conservatives, on the other hand, say the main problem is that patients do not directly pay for health care costs because medical bills are paid either by insurers or the government, causing overuse of medical services. Conservatives point to a Rand study from the 1970s, which found that patients who paid larger co-pays for health care tended to use fewer medical services. Another contributor to high costs, according to some people, is fear of malpractice lawsuits, which they say causes doctors and hospitals to order unnecessary tests and procedures to avoid being sued for not doing everything they could to make an accurate diagnosis.

Republican and Democratic senators have been unable to agree on nearly any aspect of health care reform, leading to increasingly partisan proposed solutions and legislative gridlock.

As a result, liberals generally favor cost solutions aimed at reducing the profit motive through more government regulation of health care, while conservatives often prefer solutions that increase consumer involvement in health care as well as making it harder to file malpractice claims. Many other solutions have also been proposed that involve smaller changes to the way insurance companies currently operate, including converting to electronic medical records; improving quality and efficiency in various ways; changing payment systems to reward providers for outcomes rather than each medical service; and emphasizing preventive health care services. However, the lack of agreement on cost solutions is a key reason why health care reform has been so difficult for America for so long, and why almost no proposed solutions have ever had any sort of bipartisan support (support from both political parties).

CHAPTER 3

Other Health Care Models

As the United States has continued the attempt to reform its health care policies, it is clear that the country is not alone in this struggle. Other countries have faced similar challenges. However, in contrast to the United States, which has historically allowed the private insurance market almost free rein in this aspect, most other countries have chosen to adopt some sort of national health insurance program in which the government largely provides and manages the health coverage of its citizens. There are many variations as to how other countries have accomplished this, from completely government-run single-payer systems to having a mix of public and private insurance policies available, but most other developed nations have prioritized having some sort of near-universal coverage for their citizens. The result, according to the IOM, is that, "Although America leads the world in spending on health care, it is the only wealthy, industrialized nation that does not ensure that all citizens have coverage."[23]

Health Care Models in Europe

In Europe, the push for health insurance began in the late 1800s and early 1900s, even before the United States began addressing the issue. Most European countries began by enacting government-run sickness insurance to pay workers for time lost from work when they were sick. Germany developed one of the first sick pay systems in 1883, but many other countries followed, including Austria, Hungary, Norway, Britain, Russia, and the Netherlands. Other European countries, such as Sweden, Denmark, France, and Switzerland, chose instead to subsidize worker groups that provided a similar benefit. Programs did not cover all workers at first, and they did not pay for medical services initially, but they were the beginnings of universal health insurance in Europe. Later, each European country developed its own national health care system, covering all or most citizens but reflecting each country's individual history, politics, economics, and values.

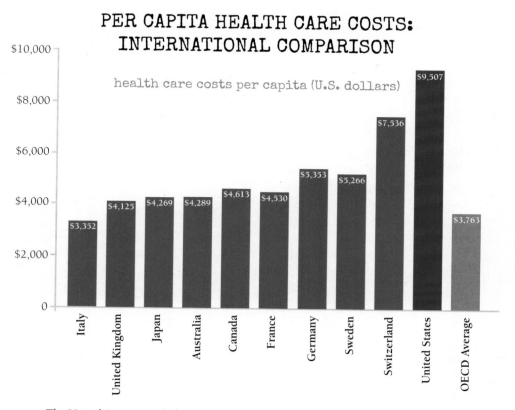

PER CAPITA HEALTH CARE COSTS: INTERNATIONAL COMPARISON

The United States spends far more on health care than other developed countries, as this information from the Organisation for Economic Co-operation and Development (OECD) shows.

According to journalist and health care writer T. R. Reid, health care systems in Europe and the world's other developed countries tend to follow one of three general models. The first model, the Bismarck (named after German chancellor Otto von Bismarck), is found in Germany, France, Belgium, and Switzerland, and has also been adopted by Japan and countries in Latin America. It is the closest to the current U.S. system. In this system, like America's system, health care providers and insurers are private entities, and the program is paid for by employers and employees. However, unlike the U.S. system, insurers are not permitted to make a profit, and costs are controlled by tight government regulation of medical services and fees.

The health care system used in Britain, Italy, Spain, and most of Scandinavia, according to Reid, is a very different model called the Beveridge (named after William Beveridge, a British social reformer). In this type of system, the government both provides and pays for all health care, financing it with taxes. Doctors are paid by the government, and clinics and hospitals are government-owned. Medical treatment is a public benefit for everyone, and no one pays out of pocket for any health care.

The third type of health care system in the developed world is the national health insurance model—a combination of the Bismarck and the Beveridge models, in which medical providers are private but the government runs the system and pays the bills with money that comes from taxes. This system is similar to the U.S. Medicaid program and is used in Canada, Taiwan, and South Korea.

The rest of the world—that is, most developing nations— uses what Reid calls the out-of-pocket system; as the name implies, people must pay for all medical services out of pocket. As Reid described it, "The basic rule in such countries is simple, and brutal: The rich get medical care; the poor stay sick or die."[24] The current U.S. health care model combines elements of all four systems, with different groups of people qualifying for different types of systems—for example, Medicare is similar to the national health insurance model and is only available to people over the age of 65. According to Reid, "All the other countries have settled on one model for everybody. This is much simpler than the U.S. system; it's fairer and cheaper, too."[25]

SOCIALISM IS NOT THE ONLY OPTION

"Contrary to conventional American wisdom, most developed countries manage health care without resorting to 'socialized medicine.'"
—T. R. Reid, author and journalist

T. R. Reid, The Healing of America: The Global Quest for Better, Cheaper, and Fairer Health Care. New York, NY: Penguin, 2009, p. 5.

A Closer Look at Germany

A more detailed review of several foreign health care systems illustrates how each of these models works. In Germany, which follows the Bismarck model, all residents are required by the government to have health insurance. Most people are covered by public health insurance; as of 2015, only about 11 percent of Germans had private health insurance. These funds are required by the government to cover everyone who makes less than $66,236 per year, and they are not permitted to deny insurance based on preexisting conditions. Only people who make more than that amount or who are self-employed are allowed to have private health insurance. The companies negotiate prices with doctors and hospitals on a local basis, and the negotiated prices then become the fixed medical price. As in America, doctors and hospitals are private and are permitted to make a profit, but by law, they cannot charge more than the fixed price. Health insurance companies are required to cover most things, but people have to pay a co-pay for certain services—such as hearing aids or speech therapy—or for things that are not considered medically necessary, such as a private hospital room. The amount each German employee pays for public health insurance is based on their income; for private health insurance, it is based on the same criteria American health insurance companies generally use, such as how healthy someone is when they apply. As NPR correspondent Richard Knox explained, "Basing premiums on a percentage-of-salary means that the less people make, the less they have to pay. The more money they make, the more they pay. This principle is at the heart of the system. Germans call it 'solidarity.' The idea is that everybody's in it together, and nobody should be without health insurance."[26]

According to most assessments, German health benefits are very generous: there are no deductibles, and all Germans get the same coverage. Moreover, health insurance is continuous, so Germans do not lose coverage when they lose their jobs; instead, government unemployment benefits pay for coverage until workers find new jobs. Because of rising health care costs in recent years, adults have to pay co-pays, but virtually all care for children is covered until they are 18 years old, even dental services. Patients also generally do not have to wait long to have surgeries or tests, and people can call a central phone number after hours and be connected to a doctor. German companies compete to provide the best benefits, offering options such as health spas, alternative therapies, and home assistance—such as cooking, cleaning, childcare, or nursing care—when patients return home after a major operation or after childbirth. As German economist Karl Lauterbach explained, German insurers compete even though they are nonprofits "because the executives earn more money, and higher prestige, if they have a larger pool of insured members."[27] This basic system has worked in Germany for more than a century.

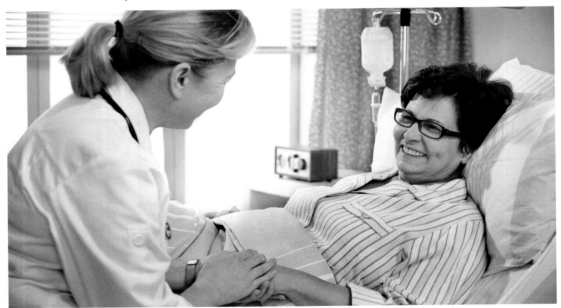

In Germany, health insurance covers most things, although a co-pay may be required for services such as a private hospital room.

A Closer Look at Great Britain

The British health care system, the Beveridge model system enacted in 1948, is an example of truly socialized medicine. Under the country's national health program, called the National Health Service (NHS), health care is provided to all by the national government and is funded by taxpayers, with no private insurers involved. The government owns the hospitals, pays the doctors, and buys all prescriptions. The central idea behind this system is that the government should provide comprehensive medical care for everyone as a fundamental social service with no fee at the point of service. As Reid described it:

> The British National Health Service ... is dedicated to the proposition that nobody should ever have to pay a medical bill. In the NHS, there is no insurance premium to pay, no co-payment, no fee at all, whether you drop by the GP's [general practitioner's] office with a cold or receive a quadruple bypass from the nation's top cardiac surgeon.[28]

This British system has been compared with the health care that America provides for its military personnel and veterans through the U.S. Department of Veterans Affairs (VA). Most British people have grown up with this system and consider it an indispensable part of British life.

The British system is considered by most health care experts to be the most cost-efficient system in the world. Because it does not need to pay for marketing or billing, for example, the administrative costs are very low. In addition, doctors are paid a set fee for each patient rather than a fee for each visit with a patient, so this limits doctors' fees. It also creates a built-in incentive for doctors to emphasize preventive care; doctors want to keep their patients as healthy as possible so that they do not come in for many appointments. However, the NHS is a massive operation, and the taxes required to pay for it are high. Many people complain that they must first see their primary doctor before they can schedule an appointment with a specialist and about the long waits to see specialists or have surgery. The NHS also controls costs by refusing to pay for some tests, procedures, and medications—a feature that many people criticize as rationing. Because of these and other criticisms, Britain passed the Health and Social Care Act of 2012. This controversial bill provides local doctors with much more influence and control over medical services and pricing, but it has been seen by many critics to be a step on the road to privatization of health care. Britain also has a small private insurance sector and private health facilities where patients can pay out of pocket or with private insurance if they are denied NHS services or choose not to take advantage of the NHS system.

Health care in Great Britain is very different from health care in the United States.

WORST AMONG DEVELOPED NATIONS

"Although the U.S. has the most expensive health care system in the world, the nation ranks lowest in terms of 'efficiency, equity and outcomes.'"
–Melissa Hellmann, journalist

Melissa Hellmann, "U.S. Health Care Ranked Worst in the Developed World," TIME, June 17, 2014.
time.com/2898403/u-s-health-care-ranked-worst-in-the-developed-world/

A Closer Look at Canada

Canada's health care is a mix of the Bismarck and Beveridge systems. First developed in the 1960s, it is publicly funded, administered by the government in a decentralized manner under government guidelines, and paid for by income and sales taxes. The system covers all Canadians regardless of preexisting conditions or income, with no co-pays or deductibles, and it generally provides preventive care, medical treatments, and a range of other services. Prescription drugs are typically covered only for the elderly and those living in poverty, but drug prices are kept low because the government negotiates prices with pharmaceutical companies. Individual provinces in Canada each develop their own health care budgets and administer the national health care program, but services are provided by private doctors and private, mostly nonprofit hospitals. Unlike the U.S. system, Canada's system is not employer-based, and although Canada has a system of private insurance companies, they are not permitted to offer plans for basic health care. Canadian insurers are limited to covering benefits not offered by the public plan, such as routine dentistry, prescription drugs, car accidents, care while traveling abroad, cosmetic procedures such as tooth whitening and plastic surgery, and private hospital rooms.

In general, most commentators agree that the majority of Canadians like their health care system. In Canada, people have access to quality care when they need it and do not go bankrupt trying to pay medical bills. However, Canadians have complained about long waits to see specialists or to have certain types of procedures. In the 1990s, Canada's Supreme Court

While the majority of Canadians like their public health care system, the accessibility of health care to all citizens can lead to long wait times for specialist visits or non-urgent procedures.

even found that some patients had died as a result of waiting for medical procedures. The government responded by providing funding to eliminate wait times for some of the most urgent procedures, such as cancer care, cardiac care, and joint replacement operations. According to some reports, however, the wait times are still long to see specialists or to get non-urgent but necessary procedures such as colonoscopies (a medical procedure in which pictures are taken of the inside of the colon to determine if there are any abnormalities). In 2016, a report by the Fraser Institute found that the average wait time for medically necessary procedures was 20 weeks, which is the longest wait time recorded since the organization began tracking the data in 1993.

How the United States Compares

During recent health care debates, conservatives have often raised fears about reforms that would make the U.S. health care system more like systems in Europe or Canada, calling them examples of socialized medicine that sacrifice the quality of care and freedom of choice available in America. These critics typically point to the wait times for medical services in Britain and Canada and claim that health care will be rationed under any type of government-run system.

Supporters of reform, on the other hand, sometimes offer unconditional praise for many of the foreign health care programs, claiming they provide superior health care and urging U.S. policy makers to adopt a similar program for America. Controversial filmmaker Michael Moore, for example, released a documentary in 2007 called *Sicko*, which emphasizes the many virtues of the government-run health care systems in France, England, Canada, and Cuba, while completely criticizing U.S. health care. As is often the case, the truth of the matter lies somewhere between these two extremes.

An independent review of the world's health care systems in 2000 by WHO ranked the United States far behind most other developed countries in the quality of its medical care. As the WHO report concluded, "The U.S. health system spends a higher portion of its gross domestic product than any other country but ranks 37 out of 191 countries according to its performance."[29]

Problems with Prescriptions

The high prices of prescription drugs in the United States have led many Americans to consider buying their prescriptions in Canada, where costs are significantly lower. The main reason prescription medications are cheaper in Canada is related largely to Canada's government-run health care system. The Canadian government sets a maximum market price on all brand name drugs sold in Canada and then allows those prices to rise only at the rate of inflation. In addition, in each of Canada's provinces, health plan regulators develop a list of drugs that will be paid for under the plan, which enables them to negotiate lower prices for some of the most popular medications. These government regulatory actions limit the amount that drug companies can charge pharmacies and other distributors of drugs, reduce the price gap between brand name and generic drugs, and protect consumers from price gouging by drug companies.

In contrast, in the United States, drug companies set the prices for the drugs they make. Of course, many companies want to make as much money as they can, so it is common for them to charge more than the drug is worth. They typically claim the prices are so high to cover the cost of researching and creating the drug, but studies have found this is untrue. Often, the research is funded by government grants, so the companies are not actually paying much for it.

Some people try to keep their personal costs down by ordering prescriptions from the internet, but according to the U.S. Food and Drug Administration (FDA), this can be dangerous. Some websites disguise themselves as reputable pharmacies but do not provide a safe or effective product. In several instances reported in 2012, people who ordered sleep aids or anti-anxiety medications "received products containing what was identified as foreign versions of Haldol (haloperidol), a powerful anti-psychotic drug. As a result, these customers needed emergency medical treatment."[1]

1. "The Possible Dangers of Buying Medicine Over the Internet," ConsumerMedSafety.org, April 6, 2012. www.consumermedsafety.org/latest-fda-medication-alerts/advice-from-fda/item/539-the-possible-dangers-of-buying-medicines-over-the-internet.

WHO's assessment was based on five indicators: overall health of each country's population; health inequalities; the responsiveness of health care providers to patient needs; how well people in all economic categories are served by the system; and whether the costs of care are fairly distributed across the population served. WHO found that the U.S. health care system is very responsive but ranks low in other categories, such as equity of care, providing care to those with less money, and financing care fairly.

A CONFUSING AND FRUSTRATING SYSTEM

"When my twins were born, one of them had to be rushed to emergency care in a different hospital, which was out of our insurance network. I could easily have had to pay $20,000 more out of pocket because of that, but I had no choice because Charlie's life was in the balance. I signed an insurance form with my baby right in front of me being wheeled away in a crazy machine. Afterward, it took four months to sort everything out. I ended up spending five hours on the phone one day, setting up six payment plans to different places to settle the nine different hospital bills we received."
–Dr. James Hampson, college professor and father of twins

James Hampson, e-mail interview, February 7, 2018.

A study by the Commonwealth Fund, a private health care research group in the United States, examined the differences in the quality of health care between selected countries using surveys of patients and doctors and analysis of other data. Its 2007 report ranked America last or next-to-last on many measures of performance. For example, the report found that all other industrialized nations provide universal care while many people in the United States lack adequate insurance coverage. The United States also ranks last in providing equitable care, since it has the greatest disparity in the quality of care provided to richer versus poorer Americans. Additionally, Americans are less healthy than people in other industrialized countries in certain categories; compared with other industrialized nations, the United States has a higher infant mortality rate, lower healthy life expectancy, and a terrible obesity epidemic. In overall performance, the United States was rated last, with poor scores for coordinating the care of chronically ill patients, meeting patient needs, and avoiding fatal surgical or medical mistakes. The Commonwealth Fund suggested that based on the report, the United States should look at how other countries handle health care and adopt some of their approaches.

A 2017 update by the Commonwealth Fund after the ACA was passed stated, "Despite the substantial gains in coverage and access to care due to the Affordable Care Act, our health care system is still not working as well as it could for Americans, and it works especially poorly for those with middle or lower incomes."[30]

At the same time, no country's health care system is perfect, and all systems have room for improvement. As a 2001 analysis by the Heritage Foundation, a conservative think tank, pointed out, problems are evident in many European health care systems. These include lack of competition among providers, limited choice of doctors, long waits for medical services, and rising health care costs for governments. Even France, considered by many experts to have the world's best health care system, faces challenges. For example, in a 2014 article for *Slate*, Claire Lundberg explained that although she was generally happy with the health care she received in France when she was pregnant, she did run into a problem when she waited too long to reserve a room at her local hospital:

> *Six weeks pregnant, I was already too late to get a spot in many of Paris' public maternity wards. Only then did I learn that most Parisian women call the hospital the day they miss their period. I have a friend who walked to her local hospital with her pregnancy test in hand the minute she found out.*
>
> *This kind of crowding, especially in bigger cities, is one of the downsides of a government-run health care system.*[31]

Since she could not get into a public ward, Lundberg had to pay out of pocket for a room in a private clinic, although her final bill was thousands of dollars less than it would have been in the United States.

The European system most often admired by conservative experts is Switzerland's—a universal system enacted in 1994 that is based on private insurance purchased by individuals, with government subsidies for those living in poverty. Premiums are not based on health risks or income; they are set according to each person's age, sex, and location. The system works through a risk adjustment system in which all insurers pay into a central fund and then are provided assistance from the fund according to the number of high-risk patients they insure. Insurers are required to offer basic health services on a nonprofit basis, but otherwise, they are free to design benefits packages and charge whatever they want. Typically, most insurers charge co-payments for medical services as well as a yearly deductible, and Swiss law prohibits patients from insuring against co-payments in most cases. This system is designed to encourage citizens to rely on private savings for a significant portion of their health care—a goal that supporters say causes patients to make more informed health care decisions and pursue preventive care and lifestyles to avoid future health risks. However, Switzerland, too, has its critics, who complain that its health care is not equitable, since everyone pays the same premiums regardless of income, and that rising health costs are making it very expensive for many families as well as for the government.

No country, therefore, has developed a health care system that suits everyone. However, it is against this background of many different but all less-than-perfect health care options that U.S. policy makers have been challenged to develop a health care system that works for America.

CHAPTER 4

Expanding the System

After nearly a century of stalled and failed health care reform attempts, the ACA was signed into law by President Barack Obama in 2010. This landmark legislation was passed after months of partisan, angry debate, and remains a controversial piece of legislation to this day, both because of what the bill actually contains and how it was passed, with almost no Republican support. There was loud opposition to the bill, both from private insurance lobbyists and Republican members of Congress, and it was a battle from beginning to end to get the necessary number of votes to pass it. Opponents of the bill promised to fight its implementation almost immediately after its passage. Supporters of the law argue that it has led to near-universal coverage for all Americans through requirements for both employers and individuals, with government subsidies put in place to attempt to make health insurance affordable. Opponents argue that the bill is killing competition in the insurance market, and that this, along with the requirement that specific medical procedures (known as "Essential Health Benefits") be covered under all plans, is driving up costs and restricting the freedom Americans have to choose the coverage they feel best suits their individual needs.

A GOOD FIRST STEP

"The Affordable Care Act is not a magic pill that will cure all the problems in our health care system ... But this law is the biggest expansion in health care coverage since Medicare."
—Kathleen Sebelius, former U.S. secretary of health and human services

Kathleen Sebelius, "Sebelius Remarks: Health Reform and You: How the New Law Will Increase Your Health Security," HHS.gov, April 6, 2010, www.hhs.gov/news/press/2010pres/04/20100406b.html.

President Barack Obama signed the ACA into law in 2010.

Runaway Health Care Costs

During the first decade of the new millennium, U.S. health care costs continued to balloon out of control. A 2007 federal report found that annual U.S. health care spending already totaled $2.2 trillion, or $7,421 per person. Despite a deep recession, which is a period of economic decline, health care costs jumped again in the next couple of years. By 2008, government reports disclosed that U.S. health care spending had grown to $2.3 trillion, or $7,681 per person—a record 16.2 percent of the U.S. economy. According to experts, this was twice the average cost of health care in other developed countries. Rising costs affected government Medicare and Medicaid spending as well as individual families. In fact, average family health care premiums had more than doubled since 2000—from $6,800 in 2000 to $12,700 in 2008—and these steadily rising premiums, combined with higher deductibles and fewer benefits, were the main reason why growing numbers of people opted to go without any type of health insurance. Not surprisingly, health care reform became a central issue in the 2008 presidential campaigns.

In fact, all the presidential candidates for the November 2008 presidential election promised health care reform, but Republican and Democratic proposals had major differences. Republican candidates Senator John McCain, former New York City mayor Rudolph Giuliani, former Arkansas governor Mike Huckabee, and former Massachusetts governor Mitt Romney generally proposed to increase insurance coverage for individuals through new tax incentives and deregulation of state insurance markets. The Democratic candidates, Senator Barack Obama, Senator Hillary Clinton, and Senator John Edwards, however, promised more sweeping reforms.

Obama's campaign, for example, pledged to create a new national health plan to cover most Americans and provide affordable health coverage similar to the comprehensive insurance provided to members of Congress. Obama said that he would accomplish this by requiring employers either to provide health care to employees or pay a penalty and by establishing a government-run National Health Insurance Exchange to help self-employed and other individuals not covered under an employer-paid health plan purchase affordable insurance. Obama's goals also included curbing insurance company abuses and cutting health care costs. Impressed with Obama's proposal, on January 28, 2008, Senator Edward Kennedy, a long-time Democratic crusader for universal health care, endorsed Obama's campaign, stating, "With Barack Obama, we will break the old gridlock and finally make health care what it should be in America—a fundamental right for all, not just an expensive privilege for the few."[32]

After he was elected, Obama made health care reform a high priority. He appointed Kansas governor Kathleen Sebelius as secretary of the Department of Health and Human Services to lead the administration's health care reform efforts, and in March 2009, he held a White House health care forum, pledging to get a health care plan passed by the end of 2009. However, instead of submitting Obama's bill to the legislature, the White House allowed Congress to develop its own legislation, and months passed with little progress and heavy partisan conflict. Finally, in a September 9, 2009, speech to Congress, Obama outlined the details of his basic plan for health care reform and asked Congress for quick action. He stated,

> The plan I'm announcing tonight would meet three basic goals: It will provide more security and stability to those who have health insurance. It will provide insurance to those who don't. And it will slow the growth of health care costs for our families, our businesses, and our government …

> Here are the details that every American needs to know about this plan:

> First, if you are among the hundreds of millions of Americans who already have health insurance through your job, Medicare, Medicaid, or the VA, nothing in this plan will require you or your employer to change the coverage or the doctor you have …

> Under this plan, it will be against the law for insurance companies to deny you coverage because of a pre-existing condition. As soon as I sign this bill, it will be against the law for insurance companies to drop your coverage when you get sick or water it down when you need it most. They will no longer be able to place some arbitrary cap on the amount of coverage you can receive in a given year or a lifetime. We will place a limit on how much you can be charged for out-of-pocket expenses … And insurance companies will be required to cover, with no extra charge, routine check ups and preventive care, like mammograms [a test to look for signs of breast cancer] and colonoscopies …

> If you lose your job or change your job, you will be able to get coverage. If you strike out on your own and start a small business, you will be able to get coverage. We will do this by creating a new insurance exchange—a marketplace where individuals and small businesses will be able to shop for health insurance at competitive prices. Insurance companies will have an incentive to participate in this exchange because it lets them compete for millions of new customers.

> As one big group, these customers will have greater leverage to bargain with the insurance companies for better prices and quality coverage …

For those individuals and small businesses who still cannot afford the lower-priced insurance available in the exchange, we will provide tax credits, the size of which will be based on your need ...

Under my plan, individuals will be required to carry basic health insurance—just as most states require you to carry auto insurance. Likewise, businesses will be required to either offer their workers health care, or chip in to help cover the cost of their workers. There will be a hardship waiver for those individuals who still cannot afford coverage, and 95% of all small businesses, because of their size and narrow profit margin, would be exempt from these requirements. But we cannot have large businesses and individuals who can afford coverage game the system by avoiding responsibility to themselves or their employees. Improving our health care system only works if everybody does their part.[33]

President Barack Obama outlined his health care plan to a joint session of Congress on September 9, 2009.

The ACA versus Obamacare

The ACA is much better known by the nickname Obamacare. This was intended to be an insult by opponents who wanted to discredit both the bill and Obama. The name stuck, and now most people are unaware its true name is the ACA—something that was proven when the late-night comedy show *Jimmy Kimmel Live!* performed a social experiment. Staffers of the show went out on the street in 2013 to ask people whether they preferred Obamacare or the ACA. The answers people gave depended on their political views: People who supported Obama tended to say Obamacare was better than the ACA, and the reverse was true for people who disliked Obama.

Throughout the 2016 presidential election process, the ACA was a major part of both candidates' platforms, so it was featured in the news often. Some news outlets called it Obamacare while others called it the ACA; reporters sometimes made it clear that these were the same program, but sometimes they did not. In 2017, *Jimmy Kimmel Live!* repeated the experiment to see if the heavy news coverage of the issue had made people aware that the programs were one and the same. However, they found many people who still believed they were different. For instance, at one point, an interviewer asked, "What is the main difference between Obamacare and the Affordable Care Act?" Obviously the correct answer would be that there is no difference, but the interviewee hesitantly responded, "One is you pay, and the other one is Obama pays ... for you."[1] This shows that many people in the United States are not well-informed about their health insurance laws.

Jimmy Kimmel (shown here) has been very outspoken about health care in the United States, especially after his son was born with a heart defect.

1. "Obamacare vs. Affordable Care Act #2," YouTube video, 3:24, posted by Jimmy Kimmel Live, January 17, 2017. www.youtube.com/watch?v=N6m7pWEMPIA.

OPPOSITION TO A SINGLE-PAYER SYSTEM

"The new health care legislation is a step toward elimination, by slow strangulation, of private health insurance and establishment of government as the 'single payer.'"
—George Will, weekly columnist for the *Washington Post*

George Will, "Let Us Disclose That Free-Speech Limits Are Harmful," *Washington Post*, July 11, 2010. www.washingtonpost.com/wp-dyn/content/article/2010/07/09/AR2010070903806.html.

Reform as a Battleground

Although ultimately successful, the process of enacting the legislation was argumentative and highly partisan. The AMA endorsed the ACA, and little opposition came from doctors, hospitals, or insurance companies, but there was a prolonged political battle between Democrats and Republicans over core issues, with Republican claims that the reforms would create "death panels" and lead to "socialised medicine."[34]

One of the fiercest fights concerned whether the health care bill should contain a public option—that is, a government-run insurance program that patients could choose instead of private health insurance. Many Democrats strongly pushed for this idea, believing a public insurance option would provide much-needed competition for private insurers and would be an effective way to control costs and stop insurance abuses. Opponents, mainly Republicans, strongly disagreed. They said cheaper premiums under a public option would likely attract so many people that the government would become too powerful, able to drive down insurance premiums to the point that private insurers would no longer be able to compete. Ultimately, opponents warned, the public option would evolve into a kind of Medicare-for-all system that could put private insurers out of business and give the government broad control over medical decisions that should be between a patient and their doctor.

In the end, to get Senate approval for a compromise health care reform bill, Senate Democrats agreed to drop the public option from their version of the legislation. Another compromise, this one made by House Democrats at the very end of the legislative process, was a deal with opponents of abortion rights that involved Obama issuing an executive order to ensure that federal money provided by the bill could not be used for abortions. This agreement helped House Democrats secure the last few Democratic votes needed to pass the final bill. Even with these compromises, the legislation passed in the House without a single Republican vote.

The passage of the ACA split the country along party lines, with those on the political left feeling it was a necessary step to ensure coverage for all Americans.

What Does the Bill Change?

Although not a radical plan, the ACA's package of reforms was nevertheless historic. As Robert Reich, a former U.S. secretary of labor and now professor of public policy at the University of California, Berkeley, explained,

It's not nearly as momentous as the passage of Medicare in 1965 and won't fundamentally alter how Americans think about social safety nets. But the passage of Obama's healthcare reform bill is the biggest thing Congress has done in decades, and [it] has enormous political significance for the future.[35]

The Congressional Budget Office (CBO), for example, estimated that the law would provide health coverage to an additional 32 million currently uninsured Americans. Although the basic structure of America's health care system—employer-based health insurance provided by private insurance companies—was not changed, the law also ended some of the worst practices of health insurance companies and attempted to lower health costs through a variety of incentives and changes. The law was structured, however, to take effect very slowly.

Initially, most Americans saw only very minor changes, with the biggest changes happening in 2014. Still, the ACA ended certain insurer practices almost immediately. For example, in 2010, it required that children with preexisting conditions be covered and that dependent children under the age of 26 be allowed to remain on their parents' health insurance policies. Also in 2010, insurance companies were prohibited from taking away health insurance once subscribers become ill, prevented from imposing lifetime or unreasonable yearly limits on benefits, required to implement a new process for appealing benefit denials, and required to provide coverage for preventive services on new plans without co-pays (and on all plans by 2018). In addition, beginning in 2010, adults with preexisting conditions would be able to buy coverage through expanded high-risk insurance pools set up by the government. The act also required a $250 rebate, or repayment, in 2010 to seniors to help them pay for prescription drugs not covered by Medicare. It was planned for this gap in Medicare's prescription coverage to be completely closed by 2020. Other immediate changes included a 10 percent tax on indoor tanning services, which have been shown to have negative effects on health, and tax credits for businesses with fewer than 50 employees to cover 35 percent of their health care premiums (increased to 50 percent by 2014).

In 2011, a number of other changes were implemented, many of them affecting Medicare. The government also helped ease the administrative burdens—the time and cost of filling out and filing paperwork—on small businesses that offer health insurance benefits and required insurers to spend at least 80 to 85 percent of premium dollars on direct medical care and efforts to improve the quality of care.

In 2013, the bill required health insurers to begin applying standards for the electronic exchange of health information to reduce paperwork and administrative costs. However, the ACA produced its most far-reaching changes in 2014. At this point, businesses with 50 or more employees were required to offer coverage to employees or pay a $2,000 penalty per employee. Moreover, insurers were no longer permitted to refuse coverage to adults who had preexisting health conditions, and they could not charge higher rates due to heath status, sex, or other factors. In addition, all Americans were required to purchase basic health insurance or pay a fine ($95 in 2014, $325 in 2015, $695 or up to 2.5 percent of income in 2016), although exceptions were to be given for financial hardship. Also, the act required states to contract with private insurers to create multistate health insurance exchanges to help individuals and small business employers shop for affordable plans. In addition, Medicaid was expanded to cover people whose income was up to 133 percent of the poverty level. People who were poor but whose income was above Medicaid levels were to receive subsidies to help them purchase insurance. These were just some of the most significant reforms; the act is extensive and implemented numerous changes.

All of this was to be paid for by the changes in Medicare and by a tax that was planned to take effect in 2022 on people who have so-called "Cadillac plans"—employer-provided health insurance plans of more than $27,500 for family coverage and $10,200 for single coverage. Also, the government planned to impose new fees on drug manufacturers, health insurance companies, and medical device manufacturers.

Potential Limits on Health Care

One of the arguments against health care reform is that it will lead to rationing, or restricting, medical care. Supporters of reform, however, often argue that the U.S. health care system—that is, the private insurance industry—already rations care by denying care to those who cannot afford to pay for it. In the future, however, soaring health care costs, made worse by factors such as the rapidly aging U.S. population, may cause the United States to eventually adopt some sort of formal rationing system. In fact, end-of-life care consumes the largest part of the Medicare budget—$55 billion in 2009. Seventy-five percent of all Americans die in a hospital, many of them in intensive care, where they are attended by multiple doctors and specialists and subjected to many expensive, high-tech tests and procedures. This end-of-life care can easily cost $10,000 per day. Many people say these efforts often do not extend life, can limit the quality of life in patients' last days, and can leave taxpayers with overpriced bills.

Conservatives argue that the ACA's creation of an Independent Payment Advisory Board (IPAB)—a Medicare cost-cutting measure—is a first step toward government rationing. The ACA establishes specific target growth rates for Medicare and charges the IPAB with ensuring that Medicare expenditures stay within these limits. ACA supporters, however, point out that the ACA specifically prohibits the IPAB from including recommendations to ration health care, raise revenues, raise Medicare beneficiary premiums, increase Medicare beneficiary cost-sharing, or otherwise restrict benefits or modify eligibility criteria. The question of rationing, therefore, is one that might not arise immediately but is perhaps one that must be addressed in the future.

"Obamacare" Branding and Other Criticisms

Following the passage of the ACA, many reform advocates praised the legislation for making a fundamental, positive change

THE BAD AND THE GOOD

"I saw people who had lost all of their teeth because adult dental care is not covered by the vast majority of programs available to the very poor ... I toured an amazing community health initiative in Charleston (West Virginia) that serves 21,000 patients with free medical, dental, pharmaceutical and other services, overseen by local volunteer physicians, dentists and others."
—Professor Philip Alston, UN special rapporteur

Philip Alston, "Statement on Visit to the USA, by Professor Philip Alston, United Nations Special Rapporteur on Extreme Poverty and Human Rights," United Nations Office of the High Commissioner, December 15, 2017. ohchr.org/EN/NewsEvents/Pages/DisplayNews.aspx?NewsID=22533&LangID=E.

in U.S. health care. *New York Times* journalist David Leonhardt, for example, praised the new law for improving equity, writing,

The [ACA] ... is the federal government's biggest attack on economic inequality since inequality began rising more than three decades ago ...

The bill ... aims to smooth out one of the roughest edges in American society—the inability of many people to afford medical care after they lose a job or get sick. And it would do so in large measure by taxing the rich.[36]

However, criticism continued from both the political left and the right. Democrats who wanted to see a public option or a single-payer system similar to Medicare complained that the new law failed to achieve this goal. In a July 29, 2010, statement, for example, Representatives Dennis Kucinich and John Conyers and Senator Bernie Sanders argued that a Medicare for All health care system in the United States still had substantial support and vowed to continue their push for such a program.

Many Republicans, meanwhile, complained that Obama's health care reforms, which they nicknamed "Obamacare," would increase costs, expand Medicaid, cause millions of people to lose their employer-provided health care, and give the federal government more control than ever over health care. As

Kevin Hasset, former director of economic policy studies at the American Enterprise Institute, a conservative think tank, argued,

> A sprawling, complex bureaucracy has been set up that will have almost absolute power to dictate terms for participating in the health-care system. That's what the law does to government. What it does to [consumers] … is worse. Based on the administration's own numbers, as many as 117 million people might have to change their health plans by 2013 as their employer-provided coverage loses its grandfathered status and becomes subject to the new Obamacare mandates. Those mandates also might make … health care more expensive. The Congressional Budget Office predicts that premiums for …
>
> families who buy their insurance privately will rise by as much as $2,100. The central Obamacare mechanism for increasing insurance coverage is an expansion of the Medicaid program. Of the 30 million new people covered, 16 million will be enrolled in Medicaid.[37]

Many Americans agreed with this assessment. According to a poll conducted by *USA Today* and Gallup shortly after the ACA was enacted, almost two-thirds of Americans said that the new law cost too much and expanded the government's role in health care too far.

Responding to his critics, Obama defended his health care plan, advertising its benefits for consumers. On June 22, 2009, the president said,

Americans on the political right felt the ACA was a serious overstep, potentially allowing the government unprecedented power over individual health care decisions.

This law will cut costs and make coverage more affordable for families and small businesses ... It's reform that finally extends the opportunity to purchase coverage to the millions who currently don't have it—and includes tough, new consumer protections to guarantee greater stability, security, and control for the millions who do have health insurance ...

Individuals and small businesses will finally have the same access to the same types of insurance plans that members of Congress have for themselves.[38]

President Obama hit the road in 2009, speaking at many town hall meetings to outline and defend his plans for health care reform.

In the years after the passage of the ACA, it has become clear that the actual impact of the program has been somewhere between two extremes: It is neither the universal health care paradise envisioned by the political left, nor is it the invasive, anti-capitalist, big-government nightmare imagined by those on the political right. It has indeed led to hugely expanded access to health care for many Americans, but there have been many problems that have arisen as a result of its implementation—some that were predicted and some that were largely unexpected. As a result, the debate regarding the need for and best implementation of health care reform continues.

CHAPTER 5

Looking Forward

The fight over the future of the ACA began before the ink was even dry on President Obama's signature. Republican lawmakers vowed to do whatever they could to limit its implementation, and lawsuits related to the constitutionality of the law were filed by states almost immediately. In addition to governmental resistance to the law, many medical and health insurance providers struggled to fully understand the complex provisions and mandates included, as well as how to meet the effective dates included. American citizens struggled to navigate the new insurance market and understand how the new mandates applied to them. Enrollment in the ACA insurance market has risen steadily over the years, but health insurance costs are also higher than they have ever been. The ideas about what is to blame for the higher costs fall, as with many other parts of the health care debate, strictly along party lines. Republicans blame the ACA itself for the increased costs, arguing that the mandates, or requirements, included in the bill have made providing insurance more expensive for private companies, as they have to pay for more costly medical treatments and are unable to charge people more money for insurance based on their individual usage of it. Democrats argue that rates were going to increase regardless and have actually increased at a significantly slower rate post-ACA than they were rising prior to its passage.

Opposition to the Affordable Care Act

The controversy surrounding the ACA did not end when it was signed into law. Soon after its passage, many Republican lawmakers served notice that they would campaign on a pledge to repeal the ACA in the fall 2010 midterm congressional elections. Also, immediately after the ACA's enactment, 28 states filed suit in federal court to protest the part of the law requiring nearly all Americans to purchase health insurance. Other legal arguments in the lawsuits claimed that the federal reform violated states' rights guaranteed by the 10th Amendment by requiring states to administer and support the law's expansion of health care and by making the federal government too powerful in the area of health care. This was ruled upon by the Supreme Court in 2012, which upheld Congress's power to enact most of the provisions of the ACA, including the mandate for people to purchase health insurance coverage.

SUPPORT FROM THE PUBLIC

"The enrollment tally [as of 2018] 'makes it crystal clear that Americans demand and support the quality, affordable health insurance and consumer protections the ACA offers,' said Robert Restuccia, executive director of Community Catalyst, a large [grassroots] health-care advocacy group."
—Amy Goldstein, journalist

Amy Goldstein, "ACA Enrollment for 2018 Nearly Matches Last Year's, Despite Trump Administration Efforts to Undermine It," Washington Post, December 21, 2017, www.washingtonpost.com/news/to-your-health/wp/2017/12/21/aca-enrollment-for-2018-nearly-matches-last-years-despite-trump-administration-efforts-to-undermine-it/?utm_term=.1b15bd7c7ef8.

In addition, about 38 states introduced legislation called the Freedom of Choice in Health Care Act in an attempt to block the federal ACA's imposition of penalties on individuals who do not purchase health insurance. However, this attempt failed.

The ACA survived these initial attacks due to favorable rulings from the Supreme Court, and its mandates were set to go into effect on schedule. After these attempts to derail the newly passed law, many experts predicted that, once the law went into full effect in 2014, the American public would come to understand and accept the reforms as being to their benefit. Pointing to polls that showed growing support for the ACA,

Shortly after the passage of the ACA, many Republican lawmakers, including Jim DeMint (shown here), expressed strong opposition to the law and announced they would be campaigning in the 2010 midterm elections on its repeal.

Maggie Mahar of the Century Foundation, a progressive think tank, argued,

[In March 2010], few Americans knew what was in the 2,500 page bill, or what impact it would have on their lives. Uncertainty fueled anxiety. But with each passing week, the public learns more about health care reform ... The more Americans learn about the details of the legislation, and how reform will help them and their families, the better they will like it.[39]

Health Care Access Post-ACA Signing

Despite the administration's efforts to portray the ACA as a vast improvement for U.S. health care, analysts looking at the details of the law raised concerns about the law's long-term effects on access to health care. Most health care experts agreed that the ACA would provide better access to health care for many Americans since it mandated health insurance coverage for millions of the uninsured, expanded Medicaid to cover an additional 16 million low-income people, and allowed parents to keep their children on their policies until age 26.

However, critics said the ACA would still leave many people with restricted access to care. Many commentators argued that the ACA would allow younger, healthier people to game the system by opting out of insurance coverage, choosing instead to pay the cheaper fine at the end of the year—until they got sick, when they could apply for coverage without fear of being denied for a preexisting condition. Largely because of this concern, John Geyman, a professor of family medicine at the University of Washington School of Medicine, predicted that by 2019, millions of people could still be uninsured or underinsured. This prediction turned out to be true; in February 2018, CNN reported that after the Republican Congress eliminated the fine completely and the administration of President Donald Trump reduced its support for the open enrollment period—moves that were set to take effect in 2019—the number of uninsured people was expected to rise by 9 million.

Other commentators worried that even currently insured people could lose coverage since the ACA allowed employers to pay a penalty instead of providing health insurance. In fact, news reports had already surfaced suggesting that some large companies were considering dropping health care coverage for their employees entirely since it would be cheaper to simply pay the penalty. Former House speaker Newt Gingrich even predicted that "the employer-based system will collapse"[40] due to this provision.

This, of course, has not come to pass. Employers that offered health insurance coverage prior to the ACA have mostly continued to offer it today. Companies use health insurance as an incentive to attract new employees; if given a choice, people are more likely to accept a job that gives them good health insurance than one that does not.

However, even though more people have access to health insurance than ever before, the number of people without heath insurance has begun to rise. According to a 2017 Gallup survey, that number rose from its record low of 10.9 percent in 2016 to 12.3 percent in 2017, although it is still far below the peak uninsured rate of 18 percent in 2013, before most of the ACA took effect. Nonetheless, it is concerning that this number is on the rise. It appears that, with the increasing cost of premiums and other out-of-pocket expenses, many young people have opted to pay the fine rather than pay for increasingly expensive premiums. As predicted, the prevailing thought seems to be that they can always go out and purchase insurance without the fear of being rejected for coverage due to a preexisting condition if they do fall ill.

In addition, people may be opting out because their insurers have largely opted out. Although most major insurers offer plans through the ACA marketplace, in recent years, several have reduced the benefits and coverage they offer through these packages. With fewer insurers competing on the government marketplace, prices have risen again, which has likely caused some people to decide not to get insurance at all.

Furthermore, there is uncertainty over the future of the ACA. President Donald Trump ran on a campaign of repealing the ACA, and he has encouraged moves to destabilize the insurance marketplaces in the meantime. These include the elimination of the fine for being uninsured as well as federal subsidies that are intended to help insurers provide coverage for low-income Americans.

However, recent figures have shown that people have not entirely given up on the ACA marketplace, despite all these issues. In December 2017, when the figures for 2018 enrollment became available, the *Washington Post* reported that although figures for 2018 were lower than those for 2017, a record was set "for the number of new consumers signing up in a single week, with 1 million such people picking health plans in the final days before the Dec. 15 federal deadline."[41] This is close to the number of people who signed up over a three-month period earlier in 2017. Despite predictions that the ACA would lose support after Obama left office and the Trump administration's attempts to create public opposition to it, the ACA is still going strong—at least for now.

ADDRESSING ONLY PART OF THE PROBLEM

"At the end of the day, [the ACA] is largely about the worthy goal of expanding access to coverage, rather than the pressing imperative of addressing explosive health care costs."
–U.S. Chamber of Commerce

U.S. Chamber of Commerce, "Critical Employer Issues in the Patient and Affordable Care Act," 2009. www.horizonagency.com/images/US-Chamber-Critical-Employer-Issues-in-ppaca.pdf.

The ACA: The Good and the Bad

The ACA has had both good and bad effects for Americans. In a 2016 article, *U.S. News & World Report* outlined some of these effects:

- Good: The ACA lowered the number of uninsured people, and many people renewed their insurance several times rather than switching to the private option, which shows that they find it to be the better choice.

- Bad: Due to negative press and glitches in the marketplace website when it first came online, which made it difficult for people to buy insurance, the law remains unpopular with many people. Additionally, satisfaction with the insurance plans offered remains low. According to the article, "Exchange plans with the lowest premiums—some as low as $75 a month—also come with deductibles that are thousands of dollars, and employers are shifting more costs to workers because health insurance is becoming more expensive and because they are anticipating federal taxes down the line."[1]

As of 2018, the Trump administration continues to push for repealing the law completely and replacing it with their own version, nicknamed "Trumpcare," rather than addressing its negative aspects.

1. Kimberly Leonard and Lindsey Cook, "Obamacare: What Went Right and What Went Wrong?," *U.S. News & World Report*, February 4, 2016. www.usnews.com/news/blogs/data-mine/2016/02/04/as-the-3rd-open-enrollment-ends-a-look-at-how-obamacare-is-doing.

Health Care Quality Post-ACA Signing

While the ACA included a number of provisions meant to improve the quality of health care, the law has also been criticized in this area. The ACA has been praised, on the one hand, for eliminating various insurance industry abuses. In addition, according to new rules issued by the government, the ACA requires insurers to pay the full cost of certain preventive medical services. According to reporter Robert Pear of the *New York Times*,

> The new requirements promise significant benefits for consumers ...
>
> The rules will eliminate co-payments, deductibles and other charges for blood pressure; diabetes and cholesterol tests; many cancer screenings; routine vaccinations; prenatal care; and regular wellness visits for infants and children.[42]

Moreover, ACA supporters pointed out that the law contains a number of provisions directly geared toward improving the quality and efficiency of the health care system. In Medicare, for example, incentives are provided to hospitals that meet performance standards for care and efficient use of resources. However, critics are not convinced that the ACA has done enough to improve quality. They point out that many people already covered by health insurance plans do not benefit from some of the ACA's insurance reforms because health insurance plans that existed as of March 23, 2010 (the date of the ACA's enactment) will be "grandfathered"—that is, exempted. According to rules issued by the U.S Department of Health and Human Services (HHS) on June 14, 2010, for example, reforms that required coverage of preventive care, coverage of emergency medical services without prior authorization, coverage of essential health benefits, and new appeal procedures do not apply to grandfathered plans. The HHS regulations, however, stated that plans lose their grandfathered status if significant changes are made to the plan that reduce benefits or increase costs to participants. According to some analysts, this means that most existing plans will eventually lose their grandfathered status and be brought into the fold of health care reform. If this did not happen naturally, there were provisions in place in the ACA to eventually bring all existing plans into line with ACA guidelines by the end of 2017. In February 2017, the Centers for Medicare and Medicaid Services (CMS) announced an extension: Grandfathered plans would be allowed to stay in place for one additional year, through the end of 2018, and then all plans must fall in line with ACA guidelines.

Critics worried that insurance companies will still find other ways to game the new law to enhance profits at the expense of patient care. As *Mother Jones* blogger Kevin Drum explained,

Starting in 2014 insurance companies will no longer be allowed to discriminate against people with preexisting conditions. They'll have to take all comers for (almost) the same price, regardless of how healthy they are.

The incentive here is obvious: within the confines of the law, insurance companies will do their best to lure the healthiest patients into their programs and convince the sickest ones to switch.[43]

At the other end of the political spectrum, conservatives argued that the biggest threat to quality care is that the ACA gives the federal government too much control over medical providers. The Cato Institute's Michael Tanner argued in 2010 that the end result of this increased government meddling in medical decisions would be a shortage of physicians. As Tanner explained, "one survey found that 45 percent of physicians would at least consider the possibility of quitting as a result of this health care legislation."[44] A loss of doctors, Tanner said, would be especially problematic, because the ACA's expansion of coverage would increase the demand for health care. However, these fears have proven to be unfounded. Although doctors may have considered quitting, in the end, most did not take that action. In fact, according to *Forbes* magazine, the United States had 100,000 more doctors in 2015 than it did in 2009. While this has not solved the shortage of doctors, it is clear that the ACA has not driven large numbers of physicians to quit.

Health Care Costs Post-ACA Signing

Whether the ACA would be able to fulfill another key goal of reform—controlling health care costs for individuals, businesses, and the government—was probably the most hotly debated question following its passage. One area of dispute was the cost of the ACA itself. The independent research agency the Congressional Budget Office (CBO) estimated that the ACA would cost $940 billion over 10 years, but because various tax increases and spending cuts offset new spending programs, the CBO estimated the law would actually reduce the national deficit by $143 billion during that period. As *Washington Post* reporter Ezra Klein explained, this means "the ACA wipes out about a quarter to a third of our long term deficit."[45] However, critics disputed these figures. According to Tanner's analysis, for example, "The Patient Protection and Affordable Care Act will cost far more than $2.7 trillion over its first 10 years of full operation, and will add more than $823 billion to the national debt."[46] As of 2018, neither of these claims has been fully proven or disproven, considering that the ACA has been in full effect for less than four years. In addition, there are many other factors to take into consideration when accounting for national debt.

Another issue brought up was the effect the ACA would have on rapidly rising costs of health insurance for employers and individuals. Many commentators have argued that the ACA's addition of new mandated insurance benefits will cause insurance rates to continue to rise even faster than before health reform because insurers will be paying out more in claims. As Tanner stated, "Most American workers and businesses will see little or no change in their skyrocketing insurance costs, while millions of others, including younger and healthier workers and those who buy insurance on their own through the nongroup market will actually see

The CBO informed Congress that the ACA would actually reduce the national deficit by $143 billion in 10 years. The truth of this statement remains to be seen.

their premiums go up faster as a result of this legislation."[47] The Obama administration promised to require insurers to justify unreasonable premium increases and to enforce the ACA requirement that insurers spend at least 80 percent of premium dollars on medical services, but, as Pear warned, "some insurers may curtail [decrease] sales to individuals or small businesses if they find the requirements too difficult to meet."[48] Critics of the ACA also complained that it would lead to huge tax increases—according to some projections, a total of $669 billion before 2019.

In fact, health insurance costs have gone up significantly since the passage of the ACA. The actual yearly cost of an employer-sponsored family health insurance premium in 2016 was $18,764, up from $12,680 in 2008, according to the Kaiser Family Foundation. Of that 2017 price, employees paid $5,714, compared with $3,354 in 2008; their employers paid the rest. Although this is a large increase, experts say it could have been larger if the ACA had not been passed. High-deductible plans are also much more common than they were pre-ACA. However, for people buying insurance on the ACA market, the average increase before government subsidies was a much steeper 25 percent, and plans were believed to increase even more in 2018.

This cannot be chalked up to the ACA alone, however. More insurers are pulling out of the individual marketplace, due to uncertainty over the future of the law and increasing uncertainty over whether or not the government will pay the promised subsidies to offset the costs of insuring low-income families. The insurers that remain are forced to increase prices to compensate. Since there is reduced competition in the marketplace in these areas, they have no real incentive to reduce prices.

ACA supporters, on the other hand, have defended the CBO budget numbers and noted the ACA's numerous cost control provisions. For example, besides the various cost-saving changes in Medicare and Medicaid, the ACA includes measures against fraud and abuse, paperwork reductions, incentives for the use of generic drugs rather than more

Senator Bernie Sanders, who ran for president in 2016, spoke frequently during his campaign about the need for a single-payer health care system.

expensive name-brand drugs, and elimination of subsidies for the Medicare Advantage program. The Cadillac tax, supporters say, provides incentives for employers and insurers to develop more cost-effective plans. In addition, the ACA includes provisions geared toward changing the way health care is delivered to make it more coordinated and efficient. In this category are provisions to encourage the use of electronic records, incentives to force hospitals to adopt practices to reduce their rates of hospital-acquired infections, and numerous pilot and demonstration projects to test cost-control ideas. Another hope is that the ACA-mandated health insurance exchanges will spur competition among insurers and lead to more affordable insurance plans.

All of these factors mean the results of the ACA are a mix of good and bad. As *TIME* magazine explained,

> *Today, Americans face higher health insurance premiums, vastly higher deductibles in health plans, and higher prescription drug costs than we ever have. But because millions more Americans have health coverage, and because things might have been even more costly had the Affordable Care Act never gone into effect, we may be better off, collectively.*[49]

COSTS KEEP RISING

"People who buy their own health plans benefited from Obamacare reforms that stopped insurers from charging sick people more or refusing to cover them at all. But like those on employer plans, they've seen their costs go up."
—John Tozzi, journalist

John Tozzi, "With or Without Obamacare, Health Care Costs Are Battering the Middle Class," Bloomberg, July 27, 2017. www.bloomberg.com/news/articles/2017-07-27/ with-or-without-obamacare-health-care-costs-are-battering-the-middle-class.

The Future of Health Care Reform

In the years after the passage of the ACA, Republicans regained control of the House of Representatives and the Senate. They got straight to work attempting to repeal the ACA once they had control of the House in 2011. They have voted on multiple measures to remove parts of the law without formally repealing it, attempting to cripple it so it would fold on its own, in addition to attempting to officially repeal it multiple times. Each time Congress passed one of these measures before 2017, it was vetoed by Obama.

These attempts became something of a running joke, and many people made comments about it. For instance, MSNBC commentator Al Sharpton joked in 2014, "If at first you don't

Controversy over New Proposals

The Trump administration has proposed many changes to the current health care system. Some of these have passed into law while others have been defeated, but nearly all have been controversial. For instance, in October 2017, Trump signed an executive order that let small businesses pool their resources to buy coverage together, extended short-term coverage policies, and allowed employers to give employees extra money to buy their own health insurance rather than covering them directly. Supporters said this would give Americans more access to affordable health insurance, while opponents said it would allow health insurance companies to offer plans that cost less but also cover less.

Another measure that has been put in place involves Medicaid. In January 2018, the CMS issued a document that allows state Medicaid directors to deny people Medicaid coverage if they cannot prove that they work or volunteer on a regular basis. Response to this has been divided. Some people believe work requirements will stop people from trying to "scam the system" by pretending to be sick so they can stay home all day and get paid by the government. They point out that other federal welfare programs, such as food stamps and unemployment benefits, have similar work requirements. However, opponents say this will hurt low-income people who cannot afford other health insurance. They noted that most people who receive Medicaid already work if they can. Those who do not are generally too ill to do so or are full-time caregivers to someone who is severely ill. Additionally, according to the website ThinkProgress, "Consumer advocates say work requirements aren't legal, and one Maine group said they'd file a lawsuit once their state's work requirement is OKed by the federal government."[1]

1. Amanda Michelle Gomez, "Trump Administration Unveils Medicaid Changes, Promotes Work Requirements for Coverage," ThinkProgress, January 11, 2018. thinkprogress.org/trump-administration-work-requirements-medicaid-d4caba28290f/

succeed, try 50 times—Republicans [are] holding a 50th vote to repeal Obamacare."[50]

Finally, after the 2016 election of Republican President Donald Trump, and after they completely solidified their control of Congress, Republican lawmakers had their best chance. Shortly after Trump took office, House Republicans got to work crafting a repeal and replace bill. After several false starts, they passed the American Health Care Act (AHCA) by a narrow 217–213 margin and sent it on to the Senate. The Senate indicated that it would not be voting on the House bill as it was and would instead rewrite the legislation. The AHCA was put to a vote in July 2017 and needed a majority of 51 Senators to pass.

MORE WORK TO DO

"PPACA is the start of a decades long process of remaking the health care system in the United States." —Wallis S. Stromberg, attorney practicing health care law

Wallis S. Stromberg, "PPACA: the Starting Point for Reform," DGS Health Law Blog, May 20, 2010. www.dgshealthlaw.com/articles/health-care-reform.

The vote proceeded largely along party lines. All 48 Democratic senators voted against it, and in a dramatic, late-night vote, 3 Republican senators voted against the bill as well, seemingly defeating the repeal of the ACA.

When asked, after a repeal bill had been pulled from a vote in the House, why the Republicans were able to pass repeal bills so many times in the past, House Representative Joe Barton stated, "We knew the president, if we could get a repeal bill to his desk, would almost certainly veto it. This time we knew if it got to the president's desk it would be signed."[51]

This sentiment was echoed by several other House representatives, including Speaker of the House Paul Ryan. They all seemed to indicate that all the votes in the past had been largely symbolic, as they knew that they would be vetoed by

President Obama, so they had never had to come up with an official replacement plan and were not prepared to be the governing party.

President Donald Trump, elected in 2016, called for the repeal and replacement of the ACA during his campaign.

There have been additional ACA repeal bills brought up as well, but as of 2018, none have had enough support to proceed to a vote. Congress, however, did pass a tax reform bill with legislation written into it to repeal the individual mandate of the ACA, which has the potential to cripple the law and collapse the individual insurance marketplaces, according to most experts. This move does not have widespread support. The bill passed in both the House and the Senate in December 2017 by a narrow margin, with all Democrats and 12 House Republicans voting no. It was opposed by 56 percent of Americans as well as the UN when it was introduced. UN Special Rapporteur Professor Philip Alston said it "will essentially shred crucial dimensions of a safety net that is already full of holes"[52] with its cuts to Medicaid and other social welfare programs.

In September 2017, Vermont Senator Bernie Sanders introduced the Medicare for All Act, which would move the United States closer to a single-payer system. However, it will be quite some time before the bill is voted on, and political experts say it has little chance of passing.

Some companies, however, are not waiting for the government to change things. In January 2018, three major companies—Amazon, Berkshire Hathaway Inc., and JPMorgan Chase & Co—said they would form a unified company to cut health care costs for their employees. According to the news website Reuters,

> The new, not-for-profit venture will initially focus on technology for "simplified, high-quality and transparent healthcare" for their more than 500,000 U.S. employees, the company said. They did not elaborate on their strategy, but said they are searching for a chief executive officer.
>
> Healthcare experts say the new entity [company] could eventually negotiate directly with drugmakers, doctors and hospitals and use their vast databases to get a better handle on the costs of those services.[53]

The future of health care is uncertain, but one thing is clear: Currently, many Americans are suffering from the high cost of health care. According to the news website Bloomberg, "Even for families without big medical expenses, health premiums cut take-home pay and their ability to save. 'It's basically robbing their future,'"[54] said Mark Kemp, a certified financial planner (CFP) who helps people understand their finances and figure out how much they need to save for things such as retirement.

If no measures are taken to change the current state of the American health care system, high prices will continue to be a burden on the average citizen. However, it is clear that there is very little agreement on what measures should be taken. Looking forward into the future, it is hard to see an end in sight to the debate over health care in America, and reform efforts will likely continue on for many years as both sides of the political spectrum attempt to push their opposing agendas.

NOTES

Introduction: An American Epidemic

1. Quoted in Steven Reinberg, *U.S. Health Care Ranks Low Among Developed Nations: Report*, Center for Advanced Medicine and Clinical Research, June 23, 2010. www.drbuttar.com/blog/?p=1229.

2. Jonathan Cohn, "When You Are Denied Health Insurance Benefits," MSNBC, October 6, 2008. www.msnbc.msn.com/id/26664727/ns/health-health_care/page/2.

Chapter 1: Understanding Health Care

3. Jonathan Cohn, *Sick: The Untold Story of America's Health Care Crisis*. New York, NY: HarperCollins, 2007, p. 6.

4. Cohn, *Sick*, p. 31.

5. Arnold S. Relman, *A Second Opinion: Rescuing America's Health Care*. New York, NY: Public Affairs, 2007, pp. 51–52.

6. Tom Daschle, *Critical: What We Can Do About the Health Care Crisis*. New York, NY: St. Martin's, 2008, p. 62.

7. Marian E. Gornick et al., "Thirty Years of Medicare: Impact on the Covered Population," *Health Care Financing Review*, vol. 18, no. 2, Winter 1996, p. 179. www.ssa.gov/history/pdf/ThirtyYearsPopulation.pdf.

8. Gina Kolata, "First Study of Its Kind Shows Benefits of Providing Medical Insurance to Poor," *New York Times*, July 7, 2011. www.nytimes.com/2011/07/07/health/policy/07medicaid.html.

9. Corinne Mitchell, "The History of HMOs," *Ezine Articles*, 2010. ezinearticles.com/?The-History-of-HMO-Plans&id=2113007.

Chapter 2: The Challenges of Health Care Reform

10. Quoted in "The 2004 Campaign; Transcript of Debate Between Bush and Kerry, with Domestic Policy the Topic," *New York Times*, October 14, 2004. query.nytimes.com/gst/fullpage.html?res=9C02EFDF163AF937A25753C1A9629C8B63.

11. Karl Rove, "ObamaCare Isn't Inevitable," *Wall Street Journal*, June 25, 2009. online.wsj.com/article/SB124588632634150501.html.

12. Rove, "ObamaCare Isn't Inevitable."

13. Alison Kodjak, "Many Dislike Health Care System but Are Pleased with Their Own Care," NPR, February 29, 2016. www.npr.org/sections/health-shots/2016/02/29/468244777/many-dislike-health-care-system-but-are-pleased-with-their-own-care.

14. Quoted in Kodjak, "Many Dislike Health Care System."

15. Philip Alston, "Statement on Visit to the USA, by Professor Philip Alston, United Nations Special Rapporteur on Extreme Poverty and Human Rights," United Nations Office of the High Commissioner, December 15, 2017. ohchr.org/EN/NewsEvents/Pages/DisplayNews.aspx?NewsID=22533&LangID=E.

16. Daschle, *Critical*, p. 3.

17. David U. Himmelstein, Deborah Thorne, Elizabeth Warren, and Steffie Woolhandler, "Medical Bankruptcy in the United States, 2007: Results of a National Study," *American Journal of Medicine*, 2009. healthcare.procon.org/sourcefiles/HimmelsteinMedicalBankruptcy2007.pdf.

18. John Daniel Davidson, "What's Better: Medicare for All, or a Free-Market Health-Care System?," *The Federalist*, March 31, 2017. thefederalist.com/2017/03/31/whats-better-medicare-free-market-health-care-system/.

19. Abdulrahman El-Sayed, "Five Reasons Free Markets Don't Work in Health Care," *Huffington Post*, April 5, 2012. www.huffingtonpost.com/abdulrahman-m-elsayed/health-care-market_b_1405396.html.

20. Cynthia Tucker, "Shouting, Stomping Won't Obscure Need for Reform," Appeal Democrat, August 9, 2009. www.appeal-democrat.com/articles/health-85291-care-consumers.html.

21. Quoted in Don Gonyea, "From the Start, Obama Struggled with Fallout from a Kind of Fake News," NPR, January 10, 2017. www.npr.org/2017/01/10/509164679/from-the-start-obama-struggled-with-fallout-from-a-kind-of-fake-news.

22. Eric Kimbuende, Usha Ranji, Janet Lundy, and Alina Salgani-coff, "Health Care Costs," Kaiser Family Foundation, March 2010. www.kaiseredu.org/topics_im.asp?imID=1&parentID=61&id=358.

Chapter 3: Other Health Care Models

23. National Institute of Medicine, "Insuring America's Health: Principles and Recommendations," January 13, 2004. www.iom.edu/Reports/2004/Insuring-Americas-Health-Principles-and-Recommendations.aspx.

24. T. R. Reid, *The Healing of America: The Global Quest for Better, Cheaper, and Fairer Health Care.* New York, NY: Penguin, 2009, p. 19.

25. Quoted in "Sick Around the World," PBS *Frontline*, April 15, 2008. www.pbs.org/wgbh/pages/frontline/sick-aroundtheworld/countries/models.html.

26. Richard Knox, "Most Patients Happy with German Health Care," NPR, August 3, 2010. www.npr.org/templates/story/story.php?storyId=91971406.

27. Quoted in Reid, *The Healing of America*, p. 76.

28. Reid, *The Healing of America*, p. 103.

29. "World Health Organization Assesses the World's Health Systems," World Health Organization, 2000. www.who.int/whr/2000/media_centre/press_release/en.

30. David Blumenthal, M.D, "New 11-Country Study: U.S. Health Care System Has Widest Gap Between People With Higher and Lower Incomes," Commonwealth Fund, July 14, 2017. www.commonwealthfund.org/publications/press-releases/2017/jul/mirror-mirror-press-release.

31. Claire Lundberg, "$200 Minus $200," *Slate*, January 27, 2014. www.slate.com/articles/business/dispatches_from_the_welfare_state/2014/01/french_socialized_medicine_vs_u_s_health_care_having_a_baby_in_paris_is.html.

Chapter 4: Expanding the System

32. Ted Kennedy, "Ted Kennedy's Obama Endorsement—Transcript," Ask Not: The Kennedy Legacy, January 28, 2008. thekennedys.wordpress.com/2008/01/29/ted-kennedys-obama-endorsement-transcript.

33. Barack Obama, "Obama's Health Care Speech to Congress," *New York Times*, September 9, 2009. www.nytimes.com/2009/09/10/us/politics/10obama.text.html?pagewanted=1&_r=2.

34. Jim Giles, "Socialised Medicine and Death Panels: Business as Usual," *New Scientist*, August 14, 2009. www.newscientist.com/blogs/shortsharpscience/2009/08/socialised-medicine-and-death.html.

35. Robert Reich, "New Health Care Bill: Biggest Change Since Medicare?," *Christian Science Monitor*, March 22, 2010. www.csmonitor.com/Money/Robert-Reich-s-Blog/2010/0322/New-health-care-bill-Biggest-change-since-Medicare.

36. David Leonhardt, "In Health Bill, Obama Attacks Wealth Inequality," *New York Times*, March 23, 2010. www.nytimes.com/2010/03/24/business/24leonhardt.html.

37. Kevin Hassett, "Obamacare Only Looks Worse upon Further Review," Bloomberg, August 1, 2010. www.bloomberg.com/news/2010-08-02/obamacare-only-looks-worse-upon-further-review-kevin-hassett.html.

38. Barack Obama, "Remarks by the President on the Affordable Care Act and the New Patients' Bill of Rights," The American Presidency Project, June 22, 2010. www.presidency.ucsb.edu/ws/index.php?pid=88087.

Chapter 5: Looking Forward

39. Maggie Mahar, "A Reply to the Cato Institute's Report on Healthcare Reform—Part 1," *Health Beat*, July 16, 2010. www.healthbeatblog.com/2010/07/a-reply-to-the-cato-institutes-report-on-healthcare-reform-part-1-.html.

40. Quoted in Rob Stone, "Progressives and Conservatives Agree: Single Payer Healthcare Is Inevitable," *Huffington Post*, August 10, 2010. www.huffingtonpost.com/rob-stone-md/progressives-and-conserva_b_676488.html.

41. Amy Goldstein, "ACA Enrollment for 2018 Nearly Matches Last Year's, Despite Trump Administration Efforts to Undermine It," *Washington Post*, December 21, 2017. www.washingtonpost.com/news/to-your-health/wp/2017/12/21/aca-enrollment-for-2018-nearly-matches-last-years-despite-trump-administration-efforts-to-undermine-it/?utm_term=.1b18bd7c2ef8.

42. Robert Pear, "Health Plans Must Provide Some Tests at No Cost," *New York Times*, July 14, 2010. www.nytimes.com/2010/07/15/health/policy/15health.html?_r=3&emc=tnt&tntemail0=y.

43. Kevin Drum, "Will Insurance Companies Game the ACA?," *Mother Jones*, August 16, 2010. motherjones.com/kevin-drum/2010/08/will-insurance-companies-game-aca.

44. Michael Tanner, "Bad Medicine: A Guide to the Real Costs and Consequences of the New Health Care Law," Cato Institute, 2010. www.cato.org/pubs/wtpapers/BadMedicineWP.pdf.

45. Ezra Klein, "OMB, ACA, CBO and the Deficit," *Washington Post*, July 8, 2010. voices.washingtonpost.com/ezra-klein/2010/07/omb_aca_cbo_and_the_deficit.html.

46. Tanner, "Bad Medicine."

47. Tanner, "Bad Medicine."

48. Robert Pear, "Covering New Ground in Health System Shift," *New York Times*, August 2, 2010. www.nytimes.com/2010/08/03/health/policy/03insurance.html?_r=2&hp.

49. Brad Tuttle, "Here's What's Happened to Health Care Costs in America in the Obama Years," *TIME*, October 4, 2016. time.com/money/4503325/obama-health-care-costs-obamacare/.

50. Quoted in Byron York, "No, House Republicans Haven't Voted 50 Times to Repeal Obamacare," *Washington Examiner*, March 15, 2014. www.washingtonexaminer.com/no-house-republicans-havent-voted-50-times-to-repeal-obamacare/article/2545733.

51. Quoted in Lee Fang, "GOP Lawmakers Now Admit Years of Obamacare Repeal Votes Were a Sham," *The Intercept*, March 31, 2017. theintercept.com/2017/03/31/repeal-votes-obamacare/.

52. Alston, "Statement on Visit to the USA."

53. Caroline Humer and David Henry, "Amazon, Berkshire, JPMorgan Partner to Cut U.S. Healthcare Costs," Reuters, January 30, 2018. www.reuters.com/article/us-amazon-healthcare/amazon-berkshire-jpmorgan-partner-to-cut-u-s-healthcare-costs-idUSKBN1FJ1NF.

54. John Tozzi, "With or Without Obamacare, Health-Care Costs Are Battering the Middle Class," Bloomberg, July 27, 2017. www.bloomberg.com/news/articles/2017-07-27/with-or-without-obamacare-health-care-costs-are-battering-the-middle-class.

DISCUSSION QUESTIONS

Chapter 1: Understanding Health Care

1. What led to the need for some sort of health insurance plan in the United States?
2. How did World War II affect the U.S. system of health insurance?
3. What does the concept of experience rating have to do with how health insurance coverage is granted in America?
4. What is managed care?

Chapter 2: The Challenges of Health Care Reform

1. Which U.S. president helped to enact Medicare and Medicaid in 1965?
2. How did the Great Depression impact health care reform?
3. Describe some pros and cons of the U.S. health care system.
4. How do conservatives and liberals differ in their views about the role of government in providing health care for Americans?

Chapter 3: Other Health Care Models

1. What is the Bismarck model of health care?
2. Describe some of the features of Britain's national health care program, and explain why it might be called a socialized system.
3. How does the U.S. model of health care differ from those of most other countries?

Chapter 4: Expanding the System

1. When was the ACA enacted?

2. Name some of the health insurance company practices changed by the ACA.

3. What does it mean to have a grandfathered plan, and what is the future of these plans?

4. Create your own health insurance plan. What do you think it should include?

Chapter 5: Looking Forward

1. What is the main claim in the state lawsuits filed in opposition to the ACA?

2. Why have efforts been made to repeal the ACA, and why have they not been successful?

3. What is the Cadillac tax?

4. Do you think that the ACA has improved health care in the United States? Why or why not?

ORGANIZATIONS TO CONTACT

American Medical Association (AMA)
330 N. Wabash Avenue, Suite 39300
Chicago, IL 60611
(800) 621-8335
www.ama-assn.org

The American Medical Association is the largest medical association of physicians in the United States. The AMA supports meaningful health care reform, and its website contains information, analysis, and articles for physicians and patients about the AMA's position on reform and the impact of the ACA.

Center on Budget and Policy Priorities
820 First St. NE, Suite 510
Washington, DC 20002
(202) 408-1080
center@cbpp.org
www.cbpp.org

The Center on Budget and Policy Priorities is a policy research organization that works at federal and state levels on economic policy and public programs that affect low- and moderate-income families and individuals. The center conducts research and analysis to help shape public debates over proposed budget and tax policies and to help ensure that policy makers consider the needs of low-income families and individuals in these debates. One of the group's main areas of research is health care, and its website contains numerous articles, analyses, and other publications about health care reform, the impact of the ACA, and other health issues.

Commonwealth Fund

1 E. 75th Street

New York, NY 10021

(212) 606-3800

www.commonwealthfund.org

> The Commonwealth Fund is a private foundation that promotes health care reform to achieve better access, improved quality, and greater efficiency—particularly for low-income people, the uninsured, minority Americans, young children, and elderly adults. The fund supports independent research on health care issues and grants to improve health care practice and policy.

National Coalition on Health Care (NCHC)

1111 14th Street NW, Suite 900

Washington, DC 20005

(202) 638-7151

nchc.org

> The NCHC represents more than 80 organizations that believe in changing the American health care system to make it more accessible, affordable, and effective.

Physicians for a National Health Program (PNHP)

29 E. Madison Street, Suite 1412

Chicago, IL 60602

(312) 782-6006

info@pnhp.org

> Physicians for a National Health Program is, as the name suggests, an organization of health professionals who advocate for a universal, comprehensive, single-payer national health program. The PNHP website is a good source for articles about health reform.

FOR MORE INFORMATION

Books

Askin, Elisabeth, and Nathan Moore. *The Health Care Handbook: A Clear and Concise Guide to the United States Health Care System, 2nd Edition*. St. Louis, MO: Washington University in St. Louis, 2014.

> This book, written by two medical students and originally self-published, offers patients information to help them navigate the complex American health care system.

Barlett, Donald L., and James B. Steele. *Critical Condition: How Health Care in America Became Big Business—and Bad Medicine*. New York, NY: Broadway Books, 2005.

> This book is a thoroughly researched criticism of the U.S. health care system.

Blumenthal, David, and James Morone. *The Heart of Power: Health and Politics in the Oval Office*. Berkeley, CA: University of California Press, 2009.

> The authors detail the history of American health care policy and discuss past presidents' attitudes toward the issue.

Schauer, Peter J. *Big Pharma and Drug Pricing*. New York, NY: Greenhaven Publishing, 2018.

> This book examines different views on how pharmaceutical companies price their drugs and what can be done to lower drug prices.

Websites

Guttmacher Institute

www.guttmacher.org

This nonprofit organization focuses on sexual and reproductive health. Its website includes articles about how federal health care decisions will affect this particular area of health care.

HealthCare.gov

www.healthcare.gov

This federal website provides answers to commonly asked questions about health coverage. It also includes the ACA health insurance exchange markets, where individuals can purchase insurance within their region.

Health Data

www.healthdata.gov

Health Data is a federal website within the Department of Health and Human Services designed to make high value data and studies related to health care accessible to researchers, policy makers, and insurance providers.

Kaiser Family Foundation: Health Care Reform

healthreform.kff.org

The Kaiser Family Foundation is a nonprofit organization focusing on the major health care issues facing the United States as well as the U.S. role in global health policy. The foundation serves as a nonpartisan source of facts, information, and analysis about health care reform for policy makers, the media, the health care community, and the public. Its website contains a wide range of information, including analyses of the ACA, issue briefs about health care matters, results of public opinion polls, and congressional testimony.

The New England Journal of Medicine: Health Policy

www.nejm.org/health-policy-and-reform

The articles in this section of the *New England Journal of Medicine*, an academic medical journal, contain expert commentary on many different issues surrounding health care reform.

INDEX

PICTURE CREDITS

ABOUT THE AUTHOR

Tyler Stevenson works for a major health insurance provider and has a strong interest in the inner workings of government. He graduated from the University at Buffalo with a degree in sociology and originally went into banking before making the switch to health insurance. He works in Buffalo, New York, and lives in the City of Tonawanda with his wife and two young daughters.